What others are s

Discov... America's Great River Road!

"Please send me Volume 1 of *Discover!* I bought two volumes in Memphis and thought, That will give me enough. It wasn't enough! You do a wonderful job of bringing the whole river experience to life!"

"We wanted to tell you that we recently made the trip from St. Louis to the headwaters. I was assigned the task of narrator, and with your books I did an excellent job! We found your guides to be most helpful. We had no problems and it was a great trip. Almost no one in our area of Texas has heard of the Great River Road. After hearing about our experiences, two couples are planning to make the trip this fall."

Having read *DISCOVER! America's Great River Road,* I cannot now imagine traveling the areas without the maps, directions, narrative background, and detailed information they contain.

"A terrific guide for those who relish boating, fishing or cruising on land along the Mississippi River."

"Three of us boated from Minneapolis to Mobile, Alabama, this past summer. We enjoyed our epic journey enormously, thanks in large measure to your *Great River Road* volumes. Your history, culture, and suggested detours were daily fascinations as we motored along at 20 mph. The kindness of strangers was beyond our most optimistic hopes. We just wanted to thank you for your good works."

Lisa Patton, Jake Callery, Silas Toulet,
Readers from Charlotte, Vermont

"I drove the Great River Road with this book at my side. When we passed out of its parameters, we felt a sense of loss."

Review, *St. Louis Post Dispatch*

"Don't leave home without a copy of *DISCOVER! America's Great River Road*. It will be a friend on the road, offering tips on things you won't want to miss as you travel the river road."

Review, DULUTH NEWS-TRIBUNE

"Last month I ordered Volume 3 of *Discover! America's Great River Road* (St. Louis to Memphis). It was Great!!! I grew up in Southern Illinois and found tons of new places to go and learned many new things about the river. I also really enjoyed your books *Wild River Wooden Boats*, *Come Hell or High Water* and *One Man the Mighty Mississippi*. Can you recommend others that are similar? Thanks for your great books!"

Dan Lindsey, Reader

Discover!
America's Great River Road
Volume 4, The Mississippi Delta

— ⚙ —

ARKANSAS, MISSISSIPPI
AND LOUISIANA

by
Pat Middleton

Pat Middleton

Great River Publishing • Wisconsin
Stoddard, WI 54658
www.greatriver.com

Pat Middleton is also the author of
Discover! America's Great River Road, Volume 1
(St. Paul, Minnesota, to Dubuque, Iowa);
Volume 2 (Galena, Illinois to St. Louis, Missouri);
Volume 3 (St. Louis, Missouri to Memphis, Tennessee);
and the ***Mississippi River Activity Guide for Kids*** (and ***Teacher Notes***).

On the Internet, visit the Mississippi River Home Page
www.greatriver.com

Published by Great River Publishing
Stoddard, WI 54658
608-457-2734
info@greatriver.com

Designed by Sue Knopf, Graffolio.

ISBN 0-9711602-1-X

First Edition, Volume 4

10 9 8 7 6 5 4 3 2 1

Contents

ARKANSAS

MISSISSIPPI

LOUISIANA

*"Like the Mississippi River,
which is seldom seen except at bridges,
commercial wharfs, and boat landings, there
is a cultural undercurrent in the Delta
that the casual visitor can't really capture
in a quick drive-through."*

Preface

Few places in North America have been as culturally isolated for as long as has the Mississippi River Delta. Traveling the Delta is an experience accented by uniquely delicious foods, vibrant jazz and blues, an uneasy truce between the great river and the sea, and the uniquely juxtaposed cultures resulting from Indian, Spanish, French, African, British, and American settlement.

It was not easy deciding where to begin this *Discover!* guidebook to the Lower Mississippi River Delta! For some, Tunica, Mississippi, just ten miles south of Memphis, Tennessee, might be an obvious choice for its proximity to Memphis and a major airport. But the Tunica casino scene is just not representative of the Mississippi River Delta. Most of us have seen glitzy casinos before. The deep southern Arkansas Delta, on the other hand, is unlike any other destination in the United States, so Arkansas is where Volume 4 begins.

The Civil War (also known in the Deep South as the *War of Northern Aggression,* the *Great War,* and the *War for States' Rights*) decimated an agriculture-based society that at its peak represented America's only native aristocracy. The landscape after the war was littered with not only the remains of magnificent plantation homes, but also the modest settlements of former slaves and sharecroppers. Today there are still families who oversee ancestral agricultural kingdoms of ten thousand acres and more. And there are still numerous descendants of former slaves; some entire families still live on the very piece of land originally allotted to their grandmother or great-grandmother!

Most official tours highlight the fabulous plantation homes (Nottaway, Oakley, Windsor, Montrose, etc.), and they are not to be missed. But the traveler should also take away an appreciation for the heart issues hiding just below the surface. Like the Mississippi River, which is seldom seen except at bridges, commercial wharfs, and boat landings, there is a cultural undercurrent in the Delta that the casual visitor can't really capture in a quick drive-through. Long stretches of cotton fields hide a rich culture of musical blues, the inequities of the "Planter Society," and the human misery caused by a rampaging Mississippi River. We saw both poverty and great wealth in extremes that are seldom seen in the United States.

So begin your journey in Tunica if you must. But remember that Tunica is not typical of the Delta you will find in the rural river bottoms. Development like that of Tunica may be a sign of the future.

—Pat Middleton

Acknowledgments

The "we" in this book generally refers to my husband, Rich, and me. It is to Rich, my good spouse and traveling partner, that I dedicate this book. While we have relied on the hospitality of many people to make our travels along the Mississippi possible, it is Rich who provides ongoing encouragement and enthusiasm. An avid history buff and a trained biologist, it is Rich's appreciation for heritage and natural history that has added perspective and vision to our travel stories for thirty-two years. Unless otherwise credited, Richard provided the photographs for *Volume 4*, including the cover photo of a grove of baldcypress trees in the backwaters of the Athafalaya River basin.

Nobody knows America's rivers better than the U.S. Army Corps of Engineers (herein referred to as *USACE*), and I have referred often to the histories of the smallest river settlements and the explanations of USACE structures as recorded in the publication *Historic Names and Places on the Lower Mississippi River.*

This Lower Mississippi River volume also would not have been possible without the guidance and generosity of the state tourism offices, especially that of Louisiana. Innkeepers made us comfortable in their inns and hotels, specialists shared their unique perspectives with us, and local guides shared their enthusiasm and familiarity with their local communities and heritage.

Finally, I woud like to note that this is the first of my Mississippi River guidebooks that will not be graciously read and reviewed by James Swift. This longtime editor, writer, and river buff died in October 2002. He is greatly missed by the entire river community.

Boardwalk at the Jean LaFitte Barataria Preserve near New Orleans.

How to Use This Book

THE ROUTE

The route suggested in this guide commences at Blytheville, Arkansas, and meanders back and forth across the river to its destination at Venice, Louisiana. In the course of our journey, we will discover, one of the top three casino destinations in the United States, and we will explore several huge U.S. Army Corps of Engineers (USACE) structures intended to tame the wild Mississippi River. We'll see miles and miles of cotton fields in Mississippi and Arkansas and sugar cane in Louisiana. In Natchez, Mississippi, we'll discover plantation mansions and *more* plantation mansions. In Louisiana we'll experience rich Creole and Cajun cultures. We'll visit the storied river towns of Helena, Arkansas; Baton Rouge, Louisiana; and Greenville, Mississippi; the National Military Park at Vicksburg, Mississippi; the bawdy French Quarter of New Orleans; and the narrow peninsular finale of the Great River Road in Venice, Louisiana.

Travel experiences along the rural river delta must be more self-initiated than in many other destinations. Locals don't realize that most visitors have never seen a sugar cane processing plant or a cotton mill. So we'll often recommend that you "ask around" for a sugar, or cotton, or rice processing plant that might welcome a visitor. A worker at the grain elevator will probably be happy to chat with you for a moment about the river that he works on every day.

We have also tried to indicate where primary overnight destinations are located. There are fewer hotels along the route than might be the case farther north along the Great River Road. Try to stay in at least one plantation home in the course of your travels, or in a B&B located in a former merchant's home—many are noted in the text. Be aware that there are long stretches without any tourism attractions, but the simple experience of seeing cotton fields disappear into the horizon or watching sugar cane burning after the harvest is key to your travel experience in the lower Mississippi River valley.

SPECIAL FEATURES FOR BOATERS

Some sites along the lower Mississippi are accessible to boaters but inaccessible to automobile travelers. We have included a "boaters only" symbol (⚓), river miles, and information about those sites. River miles are also noted in the Appendix.

ABOUT THE GREAT RIVER ROAD

The state- and federally-designated Great River Road is signed throughout the Delta with a green and white pilot's wheel, and the wheel is indicated on most state maps as well. For the most part, the route described in this book follows that pilot's wheel through each state and is designed for travelers on either side of the Mississippi River. Bridges across the river are noted in this guidebook with suggestions about what might interest the traveler on the opposite shore. Scenic easements, roadside parks, scenic overlooks, off-road parks, forests, and points of historical interest are also noted.

The Great River Road Parkway extends from Venice, Louisiana, along both sides of the river through ten states bordering the Mississippi River, to Lake Itasca in Minnesota, and continues north into Canada. Volumes 1-5 of *Discover! America's Great River Road* provide the traveler with detailed information about the heritage, natural history, and other attractions of the Great River Road. Travelers will find additional updated travel information at **www.greatriver.com,** the #1 ranked Mississippi River travel site.

Order quality travel guidebooks, river information and river history books at **www.greatriver.com/order.htm** *The Mississippi river Activity Guide for Kids,* a children's guide with teaching notes, is available for families, homeschoolers, and teachers. To order by phone, call 888-255-7726

MAPS
Each chapter begins with a regional map showing the suggested route as a heavy dotted line. Town or city maps within chapters pinpoint specific attractions noted in the text.

SYMBOLS
Special symbols identify different types of attractions throughout the guide.

⌐	Historic site	🛶	Boat launch
▲	Camping	▼	Wildlife sanctuary
🚶	Hiking	⚊	Natural area
⊼	Picnicking	•••	Suggested route
⚓	Boaters Only		

TRAVEL INSIGHTS
Each chapter includes one or more "Travel Insights"—shaded boxes giving in-depth personal, historical, or geological information.

APPENDIX AND INDEX
The appendix includes several charts and timelines as well as tourism contacts for the traveler. A detailed index is provided.

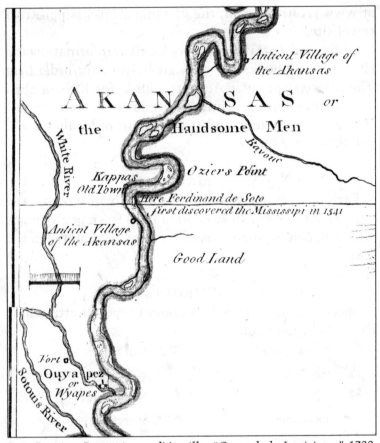

Jean-Baptiste Bourguignon d'Anville. "Carte de la Louisiane." 1732. The Tracy W. McGregor Library of American History.

ARKANSAS

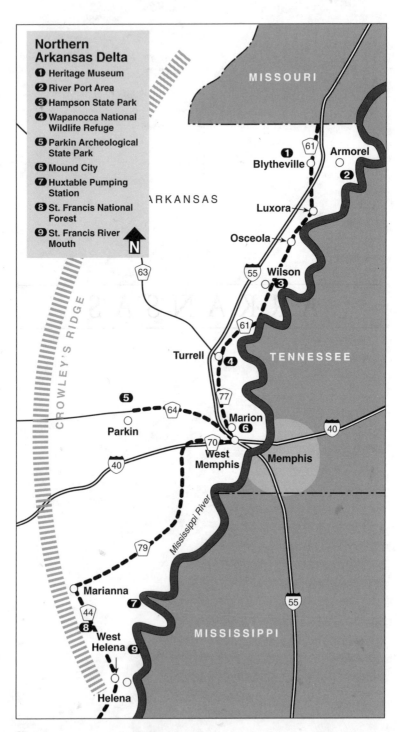

Northern
Arkansas Delta
❶ Heritage Museum
❷ River Port Area
❸ Hampson State Park
❹ Wapanocca National
   Wildlife Refuge
❺ Parkin Archeological
   State Park
❻ Mound City
❼ Huxtable Pumping
   Station
❽ St. Francis National
   Forest
❾ St. Francis River
   Mouth

N

MISSOURI

ARKANSAS

TENNESSEE

MISSISSIPPI

CROWLEY'S RIDGE

Armorel
Blytheville ❶ 61
❷
Luxora
Osceola
Wilson ❸
55
61
Turrell ❹
77
❺ 64
Parkin
Marion ❻
40
West
Memphis 70
40 Memphis
Mississippi River
79
Marianna
❼
44
❽
West
Helena ❾
Helena
55

1

Northern Arkansas Delta

The Arkansas Delta includes parts of twenty-seven counties and stretches east from Crowley's Ridge—which arcs from the northeast corner of the Arkansas/Missouri border to Helena and then to Lake Village, near the Arkansas/Louisiana border. *Arkansas* is an Illini Indian word that means "down river." Early inhabitants included Mississippian cultures and, from 1720 to the mid-1830s, the Quapaw Indian bands.

The northeastern corner of Arkansas abounds in bayous, swamps, and oxbow lakes—a legacy of the New Madrid earthquake* and the meandering habits of the Mississippi River. Flora and fauna commonly found in both the central and southern United States can be found here. Bald-cypress are abundant in the low wetlands. Spanish moss makes its appearance at Arkansas' southern border—along with spoonbill ibis and other deep south flora and fauna.

Cotton ("white gold") is king in the Arkansas delta, and fields stretch from horizon to horizon. There are no natural stones, as the bedrock is far below the rich topsoil. Before the days of irrigation, these low fields produced more cotton per acre than any other area of the country. The national cotton picking contest was held in Blytheville for many years; a prize-winning field hand might pick four hundred pounds of cotton a day.

For more on Traveling in Arkansas,
call 1-800-NATURAL or visit www.arkansas.com.

---

* For more on the New Madrid earthquakes, see Vol. 3, *Discover! America's Great River Road.*

If time is an issue, take I-55
from the Missouri border to West Memphis.
However, Hwy. 61 and several side trips
to either the river or Crowley's Ridge
will add to your appreciation of life along the river.

Whichever route you choose, do not miss
Parkin Archeological State Park,
with its excellent interpretive displays.

Follow I-55 (or Hwy. 61) to Blytheville.

Blytheville, Arkansas

Population 18,000

B lytheville (locally pronounced *blah-vul*), one of the first towns you'll encounter upon entering Arkansas on Highway 61, provides a good instant overview of life and travel in the Delta region. Like many Delta towns, it is about half black, half white, with a sprinkling of other minorities. Its population has declined steadily from 23,000 in 1996.

Yet Blytheville serves as the community center of a vast agriculturally rich region and is one of two modest delta towns well-known for its bookstore.

You'll find a number of national chain hotels in Blytheville, most located along Highway 18 at the north end of town. A stop at the Heritage Museum on Main Street helps to orient travelers to the agriculture-based lifestyle found throughout the Delta.

A BRIEF HISTORY OF THE BLYTHEVILLE AREA

T he Chicago Lumber Mill built a sawmill here to cut and process baldcypress to send to Chicago after the Chicago fire of 1871. Having clear-cut the baldcypress, the mill platted and promoted the town of Blytheville in order to sell land. Robert E. Lee Wilson, who owned much of the property from Blytheville to Wilson (30 miles south), originally arrived with one of the lumber companies. Weyerhaeuser (originally of Rock Island) still has a plant along the river nearby.

Timber and cotton were the main crops in the 1870s and 1880s. Railroads and sawmills were some of the biggest employers as tracks were laid deep into the wetlands to bring out the great baldcypress trees, many of which were thousands of years old. Barrels, shingles, and boxes were produced from the rot-resistant lumber of the baldcypress.

WHAT TO SEE IN THE BLYTHEVILLE AREA

That Bookstore

316 Main.

That Bookstore is reputed to be one of only five locations where author John Grisham *(Testament, Pelican Brief, The Firm)* will do signings. Grisham was born in Black Oak, about thirty miles west of Blytheville, and grew up in Parkin, about thirty miles west of Memphis. That Bookstore was one of the first to sell and promote Grisham's books when, as a new and unknown author, he was hand-selling his first book out of the trunk of his car.

Festival of Lights

*Between Blytheville and Gosnell. Twenty-four major motion displays easily viewed from your vehicle from the Friday before Thanksgiving until after Christmas, **www.lightsofthedelta.com.***

If you visit in December, be sure to see these elaborate lighted Christmas decorations (more than six million lights!) displayed in Blytheville, Gosnell, and the Arkansas

Aeroplex. In comparison, nearby Osceola counts 200,000 lights and Helena, farther down the river, 10,000.

In addition to a having brief stay in Blytheville, plan to explore several tiny river communities located on the flood plain between Blytheville and the Mississippi. A side trip is included on the opposite page. This is an excellent opportunity to see the working river by visiting the nearby Bunge North America grain elevator in the riverport area east of Blytheville.

Armorel

Armorel is little more than a small settlement on Highway 137. The name is an acronym for **AR**kansas, Missouri (**MO**), and REL, the initials of **R**obert **E**. **L**ee (Wilson). The town was named by one of Wilson's bookkeepers who became very wealthy in his own right.

When Wilson bought the land before the turn of the twentieth century, it was mostly swamp and was probably purchased for about fifty cents an acre. The village itself was once a consummate "company town," with every business, "from the cotton gin to the hair dresser," owned by a Wilson.

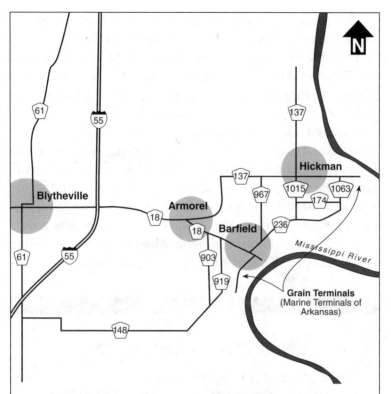

SIDE TRIP TO THE MISSISSIPPI RIVER
AND RIVERPORT AREA

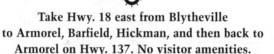

**Take Hwy. 18 east from Blytheville
to Armorel, Barfield, Hickman, and then back to
Armorel on Hwy. 137. No visitor amenities.**

Driving this loop provides a good opportunity to see small towns that originally serviced the large planters in the flood plain east of Blytheville. Arkansas Steel and several other steel processing plants are located inside the two river levees. Since 1985, the Blytheville area has been second only to Birmingham, Alabama, in steel production.

The Armorel Planting Company is still owned by the Wilson family. The corporation now mainly leases land to farmers who might plant, for example, four thousand acres half in cotton and half in grain. Early farmers would not have shipped any grain at all, selling cotton for cash and keeping the grain for horses and cattle.

Crooked Lake at Armorel was formed by the New Madrid earthquake in 1811 and 1812 (see sidebar). Delta lowlands resulting from the earthquake are now considered to be ideal for growing rice. By 1975, rice production was second only to cotton in the Arkansas Delta. Fotyeight percent of the nation's rice production is now grown in the area surrounding Helena. Most delta rice is sold to Riceland Rice, located in Stuttgart, Arkansas.

INSIGHT

New Madrid Earthquake

The quake fault lies approximately below the Mississippi River and rattled a vast area from New Madrid, Missouri, to the mouth of the St. Francis River near Helena, Arkansas. Many of the wetland areas in eastern Arkansas and northern Louisiana were formed during quakes that submerged land—land that dropped, in some cases, as much as fifty feet.

"There were no hard rocks in this section: all the country was covered by rich loams and clays, and under this surface soil was layer after layer of loose sand and clay, down to a depth of 2000 feet.

"The earth came up through these 2000 feet of sand and clay, and where breaks occurred on the surface poured streams of quicksand from deeply buried layers, veritable sand geysers."[1]

Barfield

The community at Barfield Bend was named for George C. Barfield, who kept a warehouse for unloading goods from flatboats and onto steamers. Today it lies behind the protection of the levees.

Barfield County Park

(Mile 810) On the Mississippi River off Hwy. 18, Barfield. Excellent river views, observation deck, picnic area, boat access.

Barfield, Hickman, and Huffman all began as river port towns where cotton was brought for shipping downriver.

Today, cotton is considered a "light" crop and is mostly shipped by truck rather than barge. The cotton "bales" are the size of a semi-trailer. Agriculture in northeast Arkansas today includes soybeans, wheat, and rice, in addition to cotton.

Above: Today's cotton "bales" will be shipped on trucks.

Left: Luxora historic photo: Wagons were once loaded with cotton bales at Luxora.

9

George Fielder, Grain Elevator Operator

The November morning didn't feel all that cold when we stopped to see the Mississippi River at the Bunge North America grain elevator near Barfield, but George Fielder was dressed to stay warm in the damp wind blowing off the river. The earmuffs of his wool hat were pulled tight over his ears. His full-body bib jumper was insulated, his jacket over-stuffed. We weren't there very long before the cold damp of the river began seeping into my bones.

Mostly soybeans are loaded from the Bunge grain elevators into barges. The upright elevators hold 20,000 bushels of grain each, and it takes three men to load a barge over the course of eight or nine hours. Bunge makes its own soybean oils for many fast-food restaurants. Any remaining product is sold overseas. Bunge also stores wheat, corn, and milo.

The opposite river bank is in Tennessee. Bunge located the elevator here because the narrow width of the river (about a mile) results in a deeper cut, which makes it easier to maneuver the barges.

Deer, turkey, geese, and fox might all be seen on the sandbars. Snow geese will rest on the sandbars in January in such great numbers that an open season on the geese in 2002 allowed anyone to shoot as many as they could in an effort to reduce the migrant population by about 20,000 geese. According to DNR officials, snow geese populations have exploded in the Arctic, so that the species has destroyed about a third of its habitat in the north.

Working on the towboats and barges of the Mississippi is probably one of the most dangerous jobs on the river. Here an elevator operator attends to the loading of soybeans.

Follow Hwy. 61 to Luxora.

Luxora

Population 1300

No visitor amenities.

Luxora, named for the daughter of a prominent founding landowner in the community, was once a steamboat stop called Elmot. It was replete with hotels, great houses, and merchants. When the flood of 1937 forced the removal of the town to the protected side of the levee, many of the businesses moved from here to Osceola.

Continue on Hwy. 61 to Osceola.

Osceola

Population 8,875

Mile 786, right bank descending

Highway 61 follows the levee and boasts several large mansions that once faced the Mississippi River shoreline. Osceola has shared county seat designation with Blytheville since 1901. The historic courthouse sports a copper dome, though the attractive square around the downtown courthouse is marred by empty turn-of-the-century storefronts. Shopping malls are concentrated along Highway 61. Blues recording artist Albert King is from Osceola.

Sans Souci Landing, past the Viscase plant and across the levee from the Bunge site, offers a good opportunity to see the main channel of the river. The parking, picnic area, and boat landing are maintained by the Arkansas Game and Fish commission and the City of Osceola. This landing provides the visitor with a long, wide view of the

Mississippi. Barges in the area carry wheat, cotton, and rice, among other products.

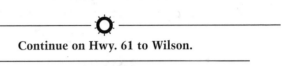

Continue on Hwy. 61 to Wilson.

Wilson
Population 939

The English Tudor architecture of this village is welcoming and totally unexpected. Robert. E. Lee Wilson, the planter for whom the town is named, originally received a land grant of 64,000 acres in eastern Arkansas. The corporation still owns 34,000 acres, most of which is leased to individual farmers.

Pecan groves in the village are owned by individual families. Pecans, while abundant in the south, require exactly the right rainfall, humidity, temperatures, etc. to be productive. Most people have one to six pecan trees for harvesting.

In 1965, Wilson's privately owned land was planted as follows: 11,000 acres of cotton, 11,000 acres of soybeans, 880 acres of rice, 3,000 acres of wheat, 350 acres of alfalfa, 40 acres of pecan trees, 350 acres of pasture, 25 acres of oats, 75 acres of strawberries, 125 acres in asparagus, 100 acres of mustard greens, 100 acres of collards, 250 acres of turnips, 100 acres of kale. The rest of the land was left fallow. In addition, Wilson leveled about a hundred acres of unused land each year for future use. The Wilson family mansion is located in nearby Victoria.

Hampson State Park

Junction of Hwy. 61 and Lake Drive. Displays include artifacts from the Nodena culture, an early agrarian Indian society in the area from AD 1350 to 1700. Gift shop and museum are open Tuesday through Saturday.

When we stopped here in December, the last three guests to sign the guest book came from Wisconsin—Green Bay, Reedsburg, and Milwaukee.

To reach the Wapanocca National Wildlife Refuge, follow Hwy. 61 to Hwy. 77 and turn left on Hwy. 77 near Turrell. Travel southeast on Hwy. 77 for two miles, turn east on Hwy. 42, go under the railroad overpass and turn right at the top of the hill (refuge entrance).

The Wapanocca National Wildlife Refuge

Adjacent to Turrell on Hwy. 77 and Hwy. 42, offers wildlife viewing and birding. Warblers can be expected in large numbers in May.

Return to Hwy. 77 and drive south to Marion. Go right on Hwy. 64 to Parkin, about 25 miles.

Parkin Archeological State Park

Located 25 miles west of Interstate 55, on Hwy. 64 out of Marion and West Memphis on the north edge of the city of Parkin, Arkansas (at the junction of Hwys. 64 and 184). The Interpretive Center and Museum Gift Shop are open 8 a.m. to 5 p.m. The archeological lab and excavations are open to the public with advance registration.

The Parkin site protects the remains of a major Mississippian culture village. It is a National Historic Landmark and is listed on the National Register of Historic Places.

The visitor/interpretive center is located in what would have been the extensive gardens—growing squash, beans, sunflowers, and acres of corn—of the native Indian village. The moat that surrounded the village is visible on the

Lt. Ross map of 1775.

south side of the site. It was perhaps 6.5 feet deep and 85 feet wide. Inside the moat is evidence of the postholes for the upright log walls—palisades—that surrounded the village. One large platform mound, on the bank of the St. Francis River, remains. As time passed, succeeding generations built on top of the ruins of the previous communities, which means that the village area itself is raised up slightly. This, in part, protected it from flooding.

This native village site was occupied from AD 1000 through the mid-seventeenth century—nearly twice as long as the United States has been a country! It served as the capital of 20 to 25 Mississippian villages along the St. Francis and Tyronza Rivers. It was only one of hundreds, if not thousands, of native villages in Eastern Arkansas. More than 1500 people may have lived on this 17-acre site.

European diseases (measles, smallpox, flu, bubonic plague) raced ahead of the white explorers to kill as much as 95 percent of the native population by the time Hernando de Soto made contact in 1541. But other factors also contributed to the disappearance of the Native culture. An increasingly dense Native population probably also took its toll in the areas of food production, the spread of native disease, local warfare, and the degradation and depletion of the environment.

INSIGHT

Hernando de Soto and East Arkansas

Although the exact route of de Soto's expedition is often disputed, the most reliable research places his Mississippi River crossing at Sunflower Bend just west of Tunica, Mississippi. According to detailed expedition notes, his small army of a thousand men first explored Florida, then South Carolina. From there, the expedition may have gradually following a route northward though Tennessee, Mississippi, Arkansas, and a brief foray through wetland swamps to the north, near present-day Caruthersville, Missouri. De Soto turned back into Arkansas to camp on the Arkansas River and planned to follow it into northern Texas,[2] but he died of fever before departing the Mississippi. To hide his death, his body was weighted and thrown into the muddy waters of the river. He has long been credited with being the first European to see the Mississippi River.

The next Europeans to appear, a hundred years later, were the French explorers Marquette and Joliet, credited with being the first Europeans to explore the upper Mississippi River.

The Parkin archeological site may have been the village of a powerful chief, Casqui. Hernando de Soto and his men met him here in June of 1541. They were the first Europeans the natives had ever encountered. Four written accounts of de Soto's expedition provide important information about Native American groups living in the southeastern United States during this time.

Continue on Hwy. 77 to West Memphis. There are many modern hotels surrounding West Memphis.

West Memphis

Population 27,666

The Southland Greyhound Park (open from April through November) is a popular attraction, while nearby Horseshoe Lake offers fishing and water recreation. A State Information Center is located on I-40 west, and numerous hotels are located off it. Just northwest of West Memphis is Mound City, the site of the sinking of the *Sultana* in 1865 (see sidebar).

Drive west on Hwy. 70 or I-40 for 12 miles and then south on Hwy. 79 for 36 miles to Marianna and the Huxtable Pumping Station.

Marianna

Population 5,263
Hwy. 79 and Hwy. 44

Marianna-Lee County Museum

67 W. Main; information on pioneer history, Native Americans in Lee County, and the Civil War.

Huxtable Stormwater Pumping Station

Hwy. 79 east out of Marianna. Turn south on Hwy. 121 and follow the signs. Tours available.

The concept of a "pumping station" is almost unknown to travelers on the upper reaches of the Mississippi. But in the South, the construction of levees to control floodwaters resulted in massive impoundments that prevent waters from draining away from fields. So *pumping* became necessary not only to prevent Mississippi floodwaters from moving into the St. Francis River, but also to pump waters impounded in the St. Francis Basin by the levees of the Mississippi and St. Francis rivers.

INSIGHT

Wreck of the *Sultana*—Mound City

It was 1865, and the Great War had recently ended. On April 15, President Abe Lincoln had died of gunshot wounds inflicted by actor John Wilkes Booth the night before while attending a performance at the Ford Theater.

Most people don't realize that about two weeks later—on April 27, 1865—America suffered its greatest peacetime naval disaster of all time. The sinking of the *Sultana*, with nearly 2,300 passengers on board, barely got a mention in the national press.

The *Sultana*, licensed to carry 376 passengers, was already carrying several hundred civilians when it reached Vicksburg, Mississippi. There, some 1,900 Union soldiers, many recently released from southern prisons, boarded the boat and were packed so tightly onto the decks that they could only stand and could hardly eat or rest.[3]

Why so many passengers were boarded has never been fully understood. Perhaps the war had fostered an attitude of risk-taking. Perhaps the captain ignored the capabilities of his boat in view of potential revenue. Perhaps a northern governor received a kickback for every soldier the *Sultana*

Continued on next page

carried—and that, a researcher suggested, was why the northern press never carried the story.

The *Sultana's* boilers exploded some seven miles north of Memphis. Most of the soldiers, enfeebled by long imprisonment, struggled only briefly before succumbing to the swift, cold currents of the Mississippi. One soldier on board wrote to his parents on April 28:

The boat had gone some 8 or 10 miles north of Memphis when she exploded. The river at the place was 1.5 miles wide with a very swift current. The pilothouse and smokestacks were all blown away and hundreds of men blown overboard, a great many scalded to death. The wreck immediately took fire; it was an awful scene. Hundreds crowded on the part not yet in flames, but all had to leave her or be burnt.

I made a leap for life then swam off. On my way I saw a great many going down to rise no more. I succeeded in finding a board about 4 inches wide, 12 feet long. The current drew me toward the Arkansas side and I landed 6 miles below the wreck on some flood wood in a cottonwood swamp. Was picked up in the morning half froze.

There was over 1,000 drowned; it was an awful sight. Some was praying and some screaming. Some that got ashore are so badly scalded that the hide all come off of them and their toenails. There was some ladies on board and small children. They was nearly all drowned. I received a small bruise on the top of my head. It is an awful thing to think of.

The *Sultana*, burning furiously, drifted down to Hen Island, in front of the little town of Mound City, Arkansas. There it sank, and river sand gradually obliterated all traces of the ill-fated boat.

When the St. Francis is higher than the Mississippi, gates are opened and the water flows by gravity from the St. Francis. When the Mississippi's level rises above that of the St. Francis, the gates are closed until the St. Francis reaches 177 feet mean sea level. The pumps then operate until the level of the Mississippi falls below that of the St. Francis.

The maximum total pumping capacity of the station is 5.4 million gallons per minute. Each of ten pumps is powered by a 3,600-horsepower diesel engine. The Huxtable station, constructed at a cost of $30 million, may be

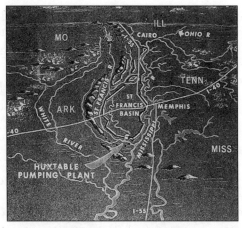

one of the largest stormwater pumping stations in the world! The watershed served by the Huxtable plant is 2000 square miles—equal in size to the state of Delaware.

From Marianna, follow Hwy. 44 into the St. Francis
National Forest, weather and time permitting.
The park is also accessible from Holly Street in Helena,
south of Marianna. Night travel through the park
is not recommended.

St. Francis National Forest

Boat landings, picnicking, campground, swimming, fishing, hunting. Storm Creek Lake at the southern entry to the park offers camping, swimming and fishing. Enjoy spring-blooming trees on a drive through the National Forest's upper and lower loops.

The St. Francis River forms the eastern boundary of the National Forest. Much of the forest serves to protect Crowley's Ridge, which is parallel to the lowlands along the river. The familiar Great River Road pilot's wheel sign appears even along the low road's gravel surface!

The St. Francis flows from the Ozark hills of southeast Missouri a distance of 475 miles to join the Mississippi a few miles above Helena. The river basin was once prone to frequent flooding, but the Wappapello Dam and Lake, constructed in 1941, now regulates much of the headwater flows. A levee nearly 300 miles long protects farmland from inundation.

The upper and lower loops of the National Forest road provide scenic relief from endless vistas of cotton and soybean in the drained areas of Delta. Trees are mostly elm, ash, sugarberry, and sweet gum.

The lower (eastern) driving loop of the forest should not be used during high water periods. At other times, it affords a unique opportunity to see native Arkansas lowlands. Baldcypress, one of the most identifiable trees in the south, crowd the edges of the river. (For more on baldcypress, see special features on page 161.) Look for low "knees" poking out of the water around the bases of trees. While it is not known for certain what purpose they serve, they most likely aid the tree in respiration in its wet environment.

The upper loop follows Crowley's Ridge. Vegetation on the upper loop is more typical of the Ozarks than the Delta, and it is possible to see coyotes and bobcats. Upland trees seldom seen in the Delta will be seen on the ridge—northern red oaks, white oaks, black oaks, post oaks and chestnuts.

Louisiana Purchase, East/West Baseline. A simple marker on the lower route notes that the baseline for the survey of the Louisiana Purchase was formed by marking an east/west line from the mouth of the St. Francis River and a north/south line from the mouth of the Arkansas River to form an intersection from which all survey points were drawn.

Storm Creek Lake Recreation Area within the National Forest offers a boat landing, picnicking, and swimming. There is a fee of $3 per car. A campground with thirteen sites is located a quarter mile north of the 420-acre lake.

Bear Creek Lake Recreation Area covers 625 acres and has 30 miles of shoreline. Picnicking, fishing, swimming, three campgrounds, a boat launch, and a 1-mile nature trail are adjacent to the lake. Marianna is six miles from Bear Creek Lake.

St. Francis River Basin and St. Francis River Mouth

Mile 672.3, right bank descending.

The St. Francis River Basin has some of the nation's most productive agricultural lands, and the effort to contain and manipulate flood waters in the low Delta regions there has been going on since 1906.

Follow Hwy. 44 to Helena.

NOTES

1 1924 *National Geographic* magazine story

2 Notes extracted from the interpretive video at Parkin Archeological site.

3 *Come Hell or High Water*, Michael Gillespie.

During our visit to Mhoon Landing, the Mississippi River was munching away at the road through the park!

Southern Arkansas Delta

❶ See Helena city map in chapter

❷ Louisiana Purchase Historic Monument

❸ White River National Wildlife Refuge

❹ Arkansas Post National Monument

❺ White River mouth

❻ Arkansas River mouth

❼ Lake Chicot State Park

2

Southern Arkansas Delta

Phillips County

When the French left the lower Mississippi Valley, Spain claimed the area, but encouraged Americans to settle by providing huge land grants to any entrepreneur willing to develop and hold his territory for Spain. William Patterson, a Methodist pastor, had established a trading post as early as 1800. Another early settler, Sylvanus Phillips of North Carolina, eventually platted a community on higher ground at the base of Crowley's Ridge. He named his community **Helena** in honor of his daughter. Phillips County is named for Sylvanus.

Prairie Point
⚓ *Mile 669, right bank descending*

Big Prairie grew up around the first log home of Sylvanus Phillips. It became a favorite stopping point for travelers along the Lower River until it was destroyed in the New Madrid earthquake of 1811 and 1812. Trees that fell during the earthquake formed a huge driftwood raft that clogged the St. Francis River well past 1836.

INSIGHT

The New Madrid Earthquake

People on board a flatboat tied to an island upriver of Memphis in December 1811 reported that they were awakened at 2 a.m. to find the earth in chaos around them.

"In a few seconds the boats, island and mainland became perfectly convulsed, the trees twisted and lashed together, the earth in all quarters was sinking, and the water issued from the center of the 25th island (Mile 801.5) just on our left, and came rushing down its side in torrents; and on our right there fell at once about 30 or 40 acres of land—some say 300 acres."*

* For more on the New Madrid earthquakes, see Vol. 3, *Discover! America's Great River Road*.

Helena
Population 7,491

Helena has long been a landmark destination on the Lower Mississippi. Mark Twain described it as "One of the most beautiful towns along the Mississippi." Before the Civil War, it was often referred to as the "Garden Spot of Arkansas." While a few bed and breakfast inns (the Edwardian Inn, the Foxglove, Magnolia Hill Inn) maintain several of the grand mansions of the past, many of the downtown homes and buildings have badly deteriorated. The Delta Cultural Center has refurbished the Moore-Hornor House, a hillside mansion near the Foxglove. Pick up a self-guided driving tour map of Helena's historic mansions at the Arkansas State Tourism Center on Highway 49.

ATTRACTIONS IN DOWNTOWN HELENA

Delta Cultural Center

141 Cherry St, on the riverfront at the railroad depot next to the levee and a separate exhibit hall across the street. Open 9 a.m. to 5 p.m. Closed on Monday and Sunday.

The Delta Cultural Center offers excellent interpretive displays on the flood of 1927, the Civil War in the Arkansas

Delta, and the march of history, from de Soto to early pioneer settlers. "Main Street Helena and the Blues" will be on exhibit through 2007.

The slough at the Delta Cultural Center and the landing on the other side is where the Delta Queen steamboats make their landing in Helena.

Blues Corner

On Cherry St.

Blues fans will want to visit this part of town, where murals on the floodwall adjacent to the Cultural Center celebrate nationally known Delta Blues musicians. Johnny Cash, Charlie Rich and Conway Twitty all had Delta roots. The King Biscuit Blues Festival, generally known simply as "da Biscuit," is held in Helena the first weekend of October. It is the South's largest free blues festival.

Helena Reach River Park

Turn east at the Doughboy statue on Cherry onto Ohio St. (right if you are coming from the Delta Cultural Center) and follow the road around the levee to a boardwalk over the river.

Planning for the boardwalk took nearly six years. Three weeks after it was built, the river began to change its course and the city lost 60 feet of its new river walk.

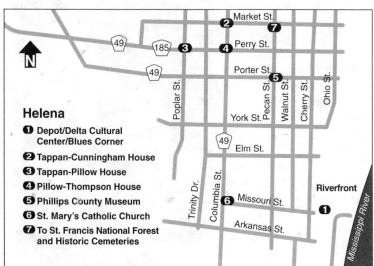

Helena

❶ Depot/Delta Cultural Center/Blues Corner

❷ Tappan-Cunningham House

❸ Tappan-Pillow House

❹ Pillow-Thompson House

❺ Phillips County Museum

❻ St. Mary's Catholic Church

❼ To St. Francis National Forest and Historic Cemeteries

The Flood of 1927

In the early 1920s, the Army Corps of Engineers boasted that its levee system had "tamed the wild river." The Delta Cultural Center display in downtown Helena noted that during this same era of confidence, the stock market was rising; Babe Ruth was hitting homeruns.

Map depicts flooded areas along the lower river in the flood of 1927.

The flood of 1927 was fed by heavy snows in the north and unusually heavy rain drenched the tributaries draining into the Mississippi River Basin. The first breach or "crevasse" of 1927 was at Mounds Landing in Pendleton, Ark. The swollen lower river then began backing up into its own tributaries so that the levees along the Arkansas River, for example, began breaking and flooding all along the Arkansas and other tributaries.

The three states devastated by this flood were Mississippi, Arkansas and Louisiana. In Arkansas, 5.1 million acres and 40,000 farms are flooded, 98 people perished. It took nearly 4 months for the flood waters to drain away. At the peak of the flood nearly 325,000 people were housed in tent camps established on river levees

After the flood of 1927, levees along the river were widened and built higher. To meet the need to control flooding, the US Army Corps of Engineers also deserted its "levees only" policy. Today, flood control on the lower river system includes a complex system of reservoirs, pumping stations, floodways, spillways.

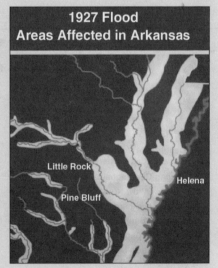

1927 Flood
Areas Affected in Arkansas

Little Rock

Helena

Pine Bluff

Tappan-Pillow House   ⚑

717 Poplar St. A private residence; not open to the public.

Although there is no documentation to support the claim, older citizens long maintained that General Sherman stayed here briefly during the Federal Occupation.

Poplar Street boasts several large homes and magnificent magnolia trees. Magnolias can live 130 to 150 years, and the oldest tree in town is that at the Tappan-Pillow House. The magnolias are evergreen. Like the southern live oak, they do shed their leaves, but never all at once, so that the tree appears green all year round.

Phillips County Museum   ⚑

623 Pecan St.; a small museum with many artifacts.

American Legion "Hut"   ⚑

Porter St.

This is the original log structure upon which many Legion lodges all over the country have been modeled. In the yard of the Legion building is a Train de la Reconnaissance or "Merci train." Forty-eight such railroad cars were delivered to each state in the Union by France after World War II as a thank you to American fighting men. It was from this gift that the 40 et 8 group evolved. Each box car was capable of carrying 40 soldiers or 8 horses or mules.

Merci Train.

St. Mary's Catholic Church
123 Columbia St.

The three virtually unknown young men commissioned to design St. Mary's went on to become world famous, each in his own field. Architect Charles Eames became one of the most important names in furniture design, his chairs selling for perhaps $20,000 each.

Emil Frei of St. Louis created the stained glass windows. During his lifetime, Frei was so well-respected that when the Vatican needed stained glass windows refurbished, it was generally Frei who was called to work on them.

Charles Quest received his first art commission when Eames asked him to produce a simple decorative mural behind the altar. Quest deliberately painted it in a very simple Byzantine style and later declared it his masterpiece. While the mural is very famous now, it caused a furor at the time it was painted, and for many years it was covered with a drape. When members threatened to paint it over, the bishop allowed a vote but stood ready to override the vote should it be in favor of repainting. The narrow vote, luckily, was to save the mural. Works painted by Charles Quest are now in permanent collections of 42 museums around the world.

Though built in 1934, the design of St. Mary's is that of an early Christian church, and the lack of windows, except for narrow slits, is noticeable on the exterior. To see the inside, request a key at the office in the Rectory next door.

Eames hired a local contractor, a Czech by the name of Vaslau Kesl, whose family had been building European churches since the tenth century. Kesl refused to put restrooms inside the church. "Whoever heard of an early Christian church with bathrooms?" he roared as he studied the blueprints. To this day there are no restrooms within St. Mary's!

Tappan-Cunningham House

Corner of Market and Columbia.

The Tappan-Cunningham House was built by a merchant who made his money in coal and railroad expansion. We found that many merchants made their fortune as southern families switched from wood-burning fireplaces to coal.

Confederate Cemetery

At the top of the hill above the main cemetery on Holly Street.

The cemetery was moved from the ridge behind the Foxglove to this high location on Crowley's Ridge. Many stones are engraved with only the words, "Confederate Dead." The United States started using dog tags after the Civil War so that soldiers could be identified in the field. There is a pleasant view of the river in the distance, and there are many magnolia trees. It is convenient to visit the cemetery if you're leaving town to drive the St. Francis River loop to Marianna.

Pillow-Thompson House

718 Perry Street, tours Wednesday–Saturday, 10 a.m. to 4 p.m.

The Pillow-Thompson House, built by Jerome Bonaparte Pillow in 1896, is one of the finest examples of Queen Anne architecture in the South.

Pillow-Thompson House.

Crowley's Ridge Geology

There was a time from 250 to 600 million years ago when an ancient ocean lapped against the limestone cliffs above the sandy beach at the tip of what we now call Southern Illinois. As eons passed, the ocean receded, leaving only a large reef in the middle of a vast flatland. The ancient Ohio and Mississippi Rivers ran on either side of the reef, but never right against it, so it didn't wear away.

As glaciers came and went, fantastic wind storms carried silt and sand from the west that blew against the reef and eventually covered it with a great thickness of fine, wind-blown soil—what we call *loess*. Today, we refer to this loess-covered reef as Crowley's Ridge, and it stretches for nearly 200 miles through the middle of the Arkansas Delta from southern Missouri to the Mississippi River near Helena. It is named after Benjamin Crowley, a soldier from the War of 1812 who founded the first settlement in this part of the state.

Crowley's Ridge gradually curves into Helena and is distinctly visible beyond the town. One of the farmers on the ridge told me that while digging a well, he hit a stump field 180 feet below the surface. The St. Francis River runs along the eastern edge of Crowley's Ridge to Helena.

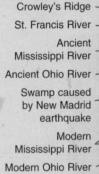
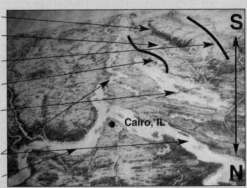

Crowley's Ridge
St. Francis River
Ancient Mississippi River
Ancient Ohio River
Swamp caused by New Madrid earthquake
Modern Mississippi River
Modern Ohio River

Cairo, IL

1862 Map of the Lower Mississippi River, looking south from the southern tip of Illinois (the Ohio River front left, the Mississippi front right). The vast lowlands created by the New Madrid Earthquake are clearly visible along the loess-covered reef known as Crowley's Ridge.

At Helena, we crossed the Mississippi and drove to Clarksdale, Mississippi on Mississippi Hwy. 1. Bridges are few and far between on the river, so if you are driving in only one direction, you'll want to note their location so you can skip to the other side of the river. Alternatively, take Hwy. 49/1 west to Hwy. 362 and the Louisiana Purchase State Park.

Louisiana Purchase State Park

Follow Hwy. 49/1west of Helena to Hwy. 362. The park is 2 miles east, where Lee, Phillips, and Monroe Counties meet.

On April 30, 1803, the Louisiana Purchase added 830,000 square miles of uncharted wilderness to the United States for a cost of $15 million. The treaty was signed by James Monroe and Robert Livingston on behalf of Thomas Jefferson and the United States.

At the park, a 950-foot boardwalk provides access to the granite monument that marks the original point from which the Louisiana Purchase was surveyed in 1815 by Prospect K. Robbins and Joseph C. Brown.

The park consists of 37.5 acres of headwater swamp that is representative of a vanishing natural environment in eastern Arkansas. In fact, this is the largest remaining headwater swamp in the entire Mississippi River Valley.

Two of the most common trees in the swamp are baldcypress and tupelo, both indicator species of a true swamp. Watch also for the swamp cottonwood, which is rarely found elsewhere in Arkansas. Today, wetlands cover only 8 percent of Arkansas's land surface.

The Louisiana Purchase.

Birding tip: Watch for the brilliant yellow-orange of the prothonotary warbler, the pileated woodpecker, shy green heron, and colorful wood ducks.

Return on Hwy. 49 to Hwy. 1 and continue south.

White River National Wildlife Refuge

Southwest of Helena and Hwy. 49. 16,000-acre refuge with more than one hundred fishing lakes.

We were told repeatedly that there was a higher population of southern bear within this wilderness area.

White River Mouth

Mile 599, right bank descending.

This tributary of the Lower Mississippi begins in Arkansas 686 miles to the northwest. It drains an area of more than 27,000 square miles and offers significant hunting and fishing opportunities. An important trade tributary, it was navigated by canoe, dugout, flat-bottomed boat, and finally a few steamboats. The USACE has maintained the navigation channel on the White River since 1961, allowing soybeans, rice, sand, gravel, limestone, logs, and other products to be shipped commercially. The **McClellan-Kerr Arkansas River Navigation System** on the Arkansas River saw four million tons of cargo moved through seventeen locks and dams and a number of lakes during its first year of operation. The system begins at the mouth of the White River and extends through a bayou into the Arkansas River about 10 miles south.

Continue south on Hwy. 1/165 to Gillett.

The Arkansas Post   ⌐■

Hwy. 165, 20 miles south of DeWitt. Visitor Center, wildlife sanctuary, driving route, museum and gift shop. No boat launches, camping, or food. The Arkansas Post County Museum en route to the Arkansas Post offers a number of rural buildings and artifacts related to county history. Small entry fee.

This is the site of the first permanent European settlement west of the Mississippi River.

A century after de Soto's expedition, French explorer Robert de la Salle visited an Indian village on the Arkansas River. He planted a wooden cross on the bank of the river and informed the natives that henceforth their lands were under the domain of the French king.

Successively, the post flew under the Spanish flag (as Fort Carlos the III), the French flag, the American flag, the Confederate flag as Fort Hindman, and finally, once again, the American flag.

At the Arkansas Post.

Arkansas River Mouth   ⚓

Mile 584.0, right bank descending.

This great tributary flows from the Rocky Mountains in the northwest for nearly 1,500 miles. It drains a vast area—160,645 square miles. Hernando de Soto crossed the Mississippi near Tunica, Mississippi, to lead his expedition to the Arkansas River, where they camped until the spring of 1542.

Arkansas River mouth by Henry Lewis.

INSIGHT

Trail of Tears Historic Trail

Bell's Route, one of three major Indian removal routes referred to as the Trail of Tears, crosses Arkansas between Memphis and Little Rock and then follows the Arkansas River to Oklahoma.

Between 1816 and 1840, Native American tribes located east of the Mississippi River, including Cherokees, Chickasaws, Choctaws, Creeks, and Seminoles, signed more than 40 treaties ceding their lands to the United States. In 1830 Congress passed the Indian Removal Act to force those natives remaining on their land to move west of the Mississippi.

Between 1830 and 1850, about 100,000 American Indians were removed to Oklahoma, often in forced marches. An estimated 3,500 Creeks died in Alabama and on their westward journey through Arkansas.[1]

Continue on Hwy. 1 to McGehee.

McGehee

Pupulation 4570

McGehee, on Highway 1, offers a Great River Road wayside park with restrooms and picnic area. Located three miles south of McGehee.

Jerome Relocation Center

One of our most unusual discoveries along the Great River Road was a monument south of DeWitt on Highway 165. It marked the site of the **Jerome Relocation Center,** one of two Japanese American internment camps located in Arkansas between September 1942 and July 1944. The Jerome site housed 6,700 American citizens of Japanese descent who were detained in temporary living quarters where community dining halls and bathing facilities were the norm. In all, more than 120,000 citizens were forcibly removed from their homes to live under the surveillance of the army in 10 such internment camps within the United States. The other Arkansas site is the **Rohwer internment camp,** north of McGehee. The Rohwer camp housed 8,500 and remained open until November 13, 1945.

Arkansas City
River mile 554.0, Hwy. 4 east of McGehee.

Arkansas City was established in the 1870s to serve as county seat for Desha County after the city of Napoleon was carried away by the Mississippi River. In 1927 a levee crevasse flooded the town to a depth of 10 feet or more and two thousand residents had to be rescued from rooftops. Today the town lies some distance from the river and miles from a major highway. Street names commemorate one famous riverboat after another—Robt. E. Lee Avenue, Natchez Street, Sprague Street, etc. There is a museum, and several buildings date from the 1800s.

South on Hwy. 65 from McGehee to Lake Village.

Chicot County

Every county seems to have some claim to fame, but Chicot County claims an often-disputed "biggie"— that the final resting spot of Hernando de Soto is in Lake Chicot. Several plantation homes are located in the county.

Chicot Landing
⚓ *Mile 565.0, right bank descending*

This is an old steamboat landing bearing the French name *Chicot*—a reference perhaps to the similarity between blackened, decayed teeth *(chicot)* and the river snags. Duck and goose hunting are popular here.

Lake Village
Population 2,791

The Arkansas State Tourism Center is located south of town on piers over the lake. It is the only tourist information center along the Lower Mississippi River that is completely heated and cooled by solar energy.

Jack R. Rhodes Lakefront Park

At the end of Main Street. Swim, picnic, enjoy the view. Walk/jog trail along the water's edge.

New Hope Baptist Church

St. Mary's Street, placed on the National Historic Register in 1986, is the oldest recorded black church in Arkansas. Organized in 1860 by Jim Kelley, a slave.

Arkansas State Tourism Center in Lake Village.

Lake Chicot State Park

2542 Hwy 257. 870-265-5480. For cabin reservations only call 800-264-2430. Fourteen cabins with fireplaces, 127 campsites with electricity and water, marina/park store. Picnicking/swimming. Self-guided Civil War tour, levee tour, bird lists. Birding, fishing (bream, crappie, bass and catfish).

Lake Chicot, at some 20 miles long, is the largest natural oxbow lake in Arkansas. There is an excellent interpretive center with displays relating to the flora and fauna of the Delta region.

The area is a nationally recognized birding destination. Trails along the levees and the lakeshore and through woodlands and baldcypress swamps offer access to various environments. More than 230 bird species have been recorded in the park and surrounding area. Expect to see large wading birds and other waterfowl. Bald eagles, and the Bonaparte's gull both winter in the area.

Spring warblers and owls are abundant in the park. In summer, watch for thousands of herons and egrets gliding in to roost for the night in the baldcypress trees along the lake. The tri-colored heron, white ibis, Mississippi kite, and even an occasional wood stork might migrate through in late summer.[5] Look for the least tern on Lake Chicot or an anhinga (a southern relative of the cormorant) drying its outspread wings. This is a large fishing bird, not a duck, thus it must dry its wings!

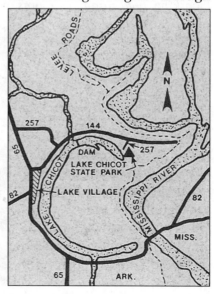

Access the self-guided Levee Tour from the parking lot at the Visitor Center. From the levees, view birds and wildlife in the burrow pits alongside. Nutria may be seen —watch for large holes around the sloughs and burrow pits where they enter their dens. Alligators may be visible in all but the winter months from the public area of the pumping station.

Lake Chicot Pumping Station: When the construction of levees began in the early 1900s, it precipitated the destruction of Lake Chicot's pristine oxbow lake. By 1985, a new $90 million pumping station, two new dams, and a diversion channel successfully imitated the natural ebb and flow of the river so well that today Lake Chicot is classified as a clearwater lake.

OTHER RECREATIONAL RESOURCES PROVIDED BY THE ARMY CORPS OF ENGINEERS AT LAKE CHICOT:

Lake Chicot Camping Area (County Park)

A 50-acre pecan orchard offers both day use and camping. 98 campsites, two boat ramps. Restrooms.

Connerly Bayou Landing Recreation Area

Picniking, boat ramp, restrooms on the lake's west side.

Ditch Bayou Landing Recreation Area

Day use facilities, 20 picnic tables, grills, restrooms, boat ramp on the lake's west side.

The Civil War Battle of Ditch Bayou, fought June 6, 1864, was the last Civil War skirmish fought in Arkansas. Vicksburg had already fallen when six hundred Confederates held off an estimated ten thousand Union troops until the Confederate soldiers could retreat. The federal troops included a Wisconsin troop from Eau Claire. This troop boasted "Old Abe," the eagle, as its mascot. Old Abe flew, screaming, above 36 battles in Missouri, Louisiana, and Mississippi, logging over 14,000 miles of travel. Southern troops called Old Abe "that Yankee buzzard" and sharpshooters in gray were always assigned to shoot him down. Old Abe survived unscathed to be retired to a two-room apartment in the Wisconsin state capitol. There he was cared for by Wisconsin veterans until dying of smoke inhalation after a fire in 1881. Today, Old Abe is remembered on the shoulder patches of the 101st Airborne Division.

Formation of Cutoffs and Oxbows

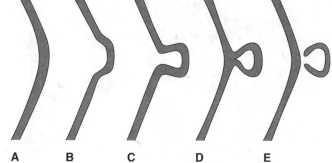

A Fast-moving water carves out land from the outer edge of the riverbank.
B Sediment is deposited along the inner bank, forming a "point" bar.
C Over time, the bend forms into a horseshoe-shaped bend.
D Eventually the river shortcuts along the narrow neck of the bend.
E Cut off from the main channel, the loop becomes an oxbow lake.

NOTES

1 *Trail of Tears National Historic Trail.* National Park Service brochure.

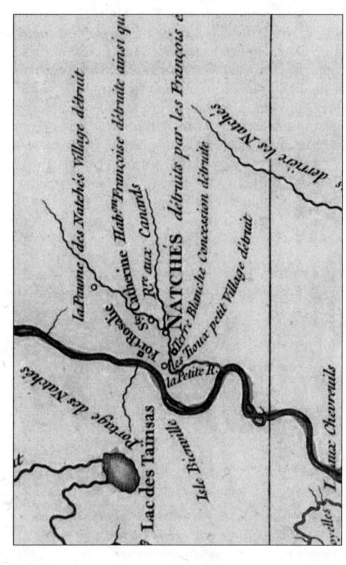

Jean-Baptiste Bourguignon d'Anville. "Carte de la Louisiane." 1732. The Tracy W. McGregor Library of American History.

MISSISSIPPI

Northern
Mississippi
Delta

❶ Mhoon Landing
Village Park

❷ Great River Road
State Park

3

Northern Mississippi Delta

A MISSISSIPPI STATE PERSPECTIVE

Many visitors using this guide will doubtless decide to launch their visit to the Mississippi River Delta by driving south on Highway 61 from Memphis to Tunica, Mississippi. With a permanent population of 9,800 and *19 million visitors* each year, Tunica is located just 16 miles south of Memphis. It is also located within a day's drive of Chicago, Atlanta, Dallas, and St. Louis. Tunica is the third most popular casino destination in the United States, so there is plenty of lodging, good food, and fun!

If the first you saw of the Mississippi River Delta was this quasi-Las Vegas "glitz" splashed over vast areas of former cotton fields, you might think that this delta is just like the upper portions of the river. But it decidedly is *not*. Outside of Tunica, the Mississippi Delta region resembles the Arkansas Delta—with a few urban civic centers, several impoverished settlements, and acre upon acre of cotton.

Civil War battles in Mississippi were fought mostly in the northern stretches of the state—from Holly Springs to Corinth and Tupelo, around Jackson, and from Vicksburg to Meridian. Before the "Great War" (a local told me it was the *only* war), Mississippi was one of the wealthiest states in the Union. The "great houses" that survived the war bear testament to that. But the Delta region has never fully recovered from the devastation of battles fought along its river shore.

A BRIEF HISTORY OF NORTHWEST MISSISSIPPI
DeSoto, Tunica, and Bolivar Counties.

De Soto, the northwesternmost county in Mississippi today, was purchased along with the land occupied by eleven other northern Mississippi counties from the Chickasaw Indian Nation in the 1832 Treaty of Pontotoc Creek. The Chickasaw were an able, warlike people who heartily disliked the French and trusted the English, often encouraged by the remnant Natchez Indians who moved into Chickasaw territory after nearly being destroyed by the French.

An exception to Chickasaw dominance in northwestern Mississippi was the Tunica band of Indians, which had settlements along the high natural levees of the Yazoo and Mississippi Rivers. These Native Americans were allies of the French, which often brought them into direct confrontation with the Chickasaw. Their descendants are currently located in the vicinity of Marksville, Arkansas.[1]

Native American history in the Mississippi River Basin is commemorated along the Natchez Trace Parkway, at Winterville Mounds Historic Site (Greenville), Grand Village Historic Site in Natchez, and Nanih Waiya (Noxapater). The Choctaw Indians, rivals also of the Chickasaw, are the only tribe still living in Mississippi. The Choctaw reservation is located near Philadelphia.

When created in 1836, De Soto County commemorated Hernando de Soto, the Spanish explorer who is traditionally believed to have been the first European to see and cross the Mississippi in Tunica County in 1541. It is believed that Tunica County might be the location of the "Province of Quizquiz" and home of the legendary chieftain, *Chisca.*

Modern-day De Soto County has benefited from the continuing growth of Memphis, Tennessee, and is highly urbanized. It is considered to be one of the ten fastest growing counties in the United States.

Tunica County

In Tunica and Coahoma County there is little debate about the pluses and minuses of bringing casinos to town: there are only pluses. In 1992, Tunica County was the poorest in the United States, with a 26 percent unemployment rate, and also rated last in education. We had never heard of the town of Tunica before this visit to the Mississippi Delta.

Today the ten themed, Las Vegas-style casinos sprawling over the former cotton fields 10 miles north of Tunica make it the third largest gambling destination in the country (after Las Vegas and Atlantic City). In 1992, 18 hotel rooms were available in Tunica; today there are more than 6,000. Unemployment is less than 3 percent, and Tunica's education system is making great strides.

Tunica Riverpark, Missisippi River Museum and Eco-Trail

Adjacent to Fitzgerald's casino. Take Hwy. 61 south to Casino Center. Turn right and drive 2.3 miles, then turn left on Casino Way. Turn right on Fitzgerald's Boulevard, then left on River-Park Drive.

This $28-million project attempts to offer a total River experience. Visitors may walk on eco-trails through a

hardwood forest and along a bayou, a levee, and other common river structures. The interpretive center provides information on the Mississippi River and the levee system. The *Tunica Queen* riverboat provides breakfast, lunch and dinner cruises.

Fitzgerald's Casino.

Tunica Historical Museum

Two miles north of Tunica off Hwy. 61 across from the Battle Arena & Exposition Center.

The museum tells the history of agriculture, the blues, Native Americans, and civil rights in Mississippi. We especially enjoyed the natural history display, the interpretation of Tunica (Woodland period) and Chickasaw Indian cultures (Mississippian period).

In traveling the Delta region, numerous locations claim to be the spot where de Soto and his troops crossed the river in 1541. John Fewkes, curator at the Tunica Museum, explained that careful scholarly research submitted to Congress in 1938 determined that only the three Tunica mounds met the exact description and juxtaposition found in the de Soto diaries. It was proved to the satisfaction of most historians that de Soto had crossed the Mississippi at a place later known as Sunflower Bend. After the Sunflower cutoff made an oxbow lake of the old bend, the lake was named De Soto Lake. A member of the expedition described the experience this way:

The river was almost half a league broad. If a man stood still on the other side, it could not be discerned whether he was a man or no. The river was of great depth, and of a strong current; the water was always muddy; there came down the river continually many trees and timber.

"The old research was done with a spirit of following the evidence to wherever it led," Fewkes explained, "while much modern research is focused on proving a theory for economic purposes (often to promote regional tourism). I prefer to believe the original research unless new information forces a significant change of thought."

Tunica County offers excellent outdoor recreation. Nash Buckingham, a well-known waterfowler and outdoors writer, used his beloved Beaver Dam Lake as the location of many of his hunting stories including *De Shootinest Gent'man*, available in the Museum Shop. Beaver Dam Lake is about 4 miles south of Tunica. Tunica Lake offers good year-round fishing with easy access for boats.

Town of Tunica

The *old town* of Tunica sits 26 miles south of the Tennessee-Misssissippi state line, about 10 miles south of the casinos and about 32 miles north of Clarksdale. The Tate Log House a dogtrot style log cabin built in 1841, is the oldest structure in the town. The north-south railroad corridor (roughly along today's Highway 61) opened an alternative to river travel when inland roads were basically nonexistent.

It is clear that Tunica has benefited greatly from casino gaming revenues. The 1923 Tunica County Court House is recently refurbished. Historic Downtown Tunica is a well-preserved and rejuvenated, with many antique stores, gift shops, and an old-fashioned deli and ice cream parlor. Even the sidewalks have been restored to the historic two-levels once typical of southern towns.

Tunica Welcome Center

Corner of Magnolia and School Streets in the Tate Log House. Tourism information is available online at tunicamainstreet.com, tunicachamber.com and tunicamuseum.com

Rivergate Park

Downtown Tunica.

Rivergate Park is home of the poignant Veterans Memorial. The railroad depot that once sat in the center boulevard at the south end of town is gone, but a small city park now features a bronze statue of three Vietnam War soldiers and a memorial plaque for each major U.S. war (except the Civil War).

Rivergate is also the home of the annual **Rivergate Barbecue Festival** in April and the **Tunica Gospel Festival** in October.

The Hotel Marie and Café (1881)

Historic downtown Tunica

This structure was recently restored for use as an upscale hotel after long service as a traveler's rest, brothel, washeteria, and grocery store. It offers rooms, meals, and a cozy bar, and contains the offices of the Tunica County Chamber of Commerce.

Bronze war statue in Rivergate Park.

Blue and White Café

Corner of Rt. 4 and Hwy. 61

A popular café, the Blue and White was reputed to have been a favorite of Elvis Presley.

Mhoon Landing Village Park ⛏

Scenic Drive, Mile 687.6. Follow Hwy. 4 west past the Hotel Marie (downtown) into the cotton fields that surround Tunica. Turn right to follow the paved road between the Tunica Levee Inn and a small cemetery.

This 5-mile scenic drive provides a quick overview of the Delta landscape and a rare close-up view of the Mississippi River. At the time of our visit, the road in the park simply ended where the river had eaten away a huge chunk of the riverbank. Such cuts reveal that the rich topsoil in northern Mississippi is 40 to 60 feet deep. The park was named after Chief Mhoon, an Indian landowner in the area.

To get to the village park at Mhoon Landing, you must drive over the great **Yazoo-Mississippi Delta Levee** that protects the county's farm fields from the ravages of the river when in flood. The outer levee is 40 feet high and was constructed during the Great Depression as a WPA project that brought jobs to the area. Inside is a second levee that was constructed after the flood of 1927. The levee on the left descending bank of the Mississippi River from Tennessee to Vicksburg is privately maintained by a citizen organization, and each property owner is taxed for levee maintenance.

The park at Mhoon Landing offers picnic tables and an unobstructed view of a broad bend of the Mississippi River. Listen for the constant chatter of the river as it tumbles upon itself rushing by the bend. This is not the sound of wind in the trees or the noise of traffic. This is the river. A wire denotes the edge of the rock riprap and concrete revetment that extends along the entire bend to prevent the river from continuing to move ever more eastward.

A sign threatens a $500 fine for walking onto the revetment or riprap. This is not a pleasure river, but seething brown muscle. Don't even think of going beyond the wire!

**Continue on Hwy. 61 to Hwy. 49.
Turn right and then left
on Hwy. 1 to Friar's Point.**

INSIGHT

Mississippi River Stats at Mhoon Landing

Width, bank to bank: 1 mile; depth: generally 50 to 60 feet, though river levels can vary by as much as 40 feet. The navigation channel is about 300 feet wide; the current is 4 to 6 miles per hour but can increase to 10 miles per hour in flood. The average daily flow into the Gulf of Mexico is 300 billion gallons—600 billion gallons in flood. The drainage area is 1.25 million square miles, nearly 40 percent of the entire United States, including parts of 31 states. Length is 2,400 miles. From Cairo Point to the Gulf is about 950 river miles or 475 air miles. The river at Mhoon Landing is about 162 feet above sea level. The major tributaries are the Missouri, the Ohio, the Illinois, the Cumberland, the Arkansas, and the Tennessee. These rivers provide over 15,000 miles of navigable waterways. It is estimated that the towboats on the river move nearly 500 million tons of freight annually.[2]

Friars Point
River mile 652.

Like so many small towns along the lower river, Friars Point declined rapidly after the Civil War. But it flourished as a county seat before the Civil War, when it replaced Delta, Mississippi, as the seat of government. Today the county seat has moved inland, and Friars Point lies behind the main levee. It has an small, eclectic museum and several empty stores. The Reverend C. L. Franklin once preached at the little church. His daughter Aretha was in the choir!

Uncle Henry's B&B

Go south on Hwy. 61 to the intersection with Hwy. 49, then 2.3 miles west. 5860 Moon Lake Road. Call for room or dinner reservations, 601-337-2757.

Uncle Henry's is recommended for good Cajun cooking. Known as the Moon Lake Club in the 1930s and '40s, it appears in the works of both Tennessee Williams and William Faulkner.

Belle Clark B&B

Clarksdale.

The Belle Clark includes four rooms in the original home of John & Eliza Clark for whom Clarksdale is named, and three rooms in the old schoolhouse.

Take Friars Point Road east out of Friars Point to Clarksdale.

The Flood of 1927

A large photograph of the Mounds at Greenville shows the area during the flood of 1927. One of 13 major crevasses in the levee system occurred just seven miles below Mhoon Landing at Whitehall on the Arkansas bank. Once breached, the crevasse rapidly grew to 2,400 feet and nearly joined the St. Francis River and the Mississippi several miles above its current mouth. Had the levee crevasses not occurred, the flooded river would have overtopped the 1927 levee by four feet. In total, official reports estimate that 330,000 persons had to be rescued from trees and housetops and 700,000 people throughout the Delta region had to leave their homes.

Clarksdale

As we drove toward Clarksdale, a tidy collection of humanity in the center of endless cotton fields, Rich asked me why I had chosen this town to spend the night in. His question was briefly disconcerting!

"BLUES!" I said abruptly, as it came to mind. "I was hoping we might have some good food and listen to some live blues. That would be kind of different and . . . fun."

"Oh, it will be," he assured me gallantly. "I'd like that."

Well, blues weren't happening in Clarksdale on a Wednesday night, it turned out. In fact, anyone counting on hearing live blues had best call ahead. Chances are good that a number of performers will be hanging out, but this happens mostly on weekends and Thursday nights. Call the Clarksdale Chamber of Commerce or 800-626-3764 (the Delta Blues Museum) for more information.

So we heard no blues, but we did enjoy one carefully dilapidated and upscale "blues joint" called Ground Zero located near the Delta Blues Museum. Ground Zero and another decidedly upscale restaurant, Madidi, are both are owned by Morgan Freeman.

Morgan Freeman? Turns out that when he's not working in movies, he lives in nearby Charleston. We found out that Muddy Waters, Tennessee Williams, W. C. Handy, Charlie Patton, John Lee Hooker, and any number of other famous artists have also called the Clarksdale area home.

"It's the cotton fields," we were told. "We have cotton fields, and where there's cotton, there's blues."

Blues fans will want to drive along Sunflower Avenue along the Sunflower riverfront (the Sunflower River flows through town). Riverside Hotel, another classic blues landmark, was originally Clarksdale's black hospital. Bessie Smith, "Empress of the Blues," died there in 1937. John Kennedy, Jr., stopped here on his tour of the Delta in 1991.

Standing on Delta Avenue, in a 1940s kind of downtown, there are no cotton fields to be seen. The cotton fields we *have* seen remind even me of endless labor, and it's restful not to see them for a while. It occurs to me that a trip to town might have comforted the field hands in a similar way. A two-story building blocked out the fields for a few hours. They could look at shop windows, dream about being somewhere else, eat a little, drink a little, sing a little. And that's why there's the blues.

What else to see? The **Delta Blues Museum** at 1 Blues Alley for sure, and a cool little shop downtown called **Cat Head Delta Blues & Folk Art, Inc.** There we found eclectic art, blues CDs, river books, and more at 114 Delta Avenue. If you, too, miss the "real thing," tune in to the blues station, WROX, at 1450 AM.

Cat Head Delta Blues & Folk Art, Inc.

SPECIAL EVENTS IN CLARKSDALE

Tennessee Williams Festival

October.

This festival celebrates Clarksdale's ties to Williams, who spent his childhood here. Much of his writing was based on characters similar to those he knew as a child. Mrs. Wingfield, a friend of his grandfather, was immortalized in *The Glass Menagerie*. The Moon Lake Casino, now Uncle Henry's Place & Inn, played a part in several of his plays. The old Alcazar Hotel was the scene of Alma Winemiller's adventures in two of his plays, while the Cutrer Mansion at 109 Clark St. was the original home of Blanche Clark Cutrer in *A Streetcar Named Desire*. The festival features a drama competition, a "Stella" calling contest, lectures, workshops, a walking tour, and dinners at several favorite Williams locales.

Sunflower River Blues and Gospel Festival

August. Phone 662-627-7337 for more information.

This festival offers the best in contemporary blues and gospel music. It is considered to be one of the purest blues festivals in the south.

For more information on festivals or B&Bs in Clarksdale, contact Coahoma County Tourism Commission, 800-626-3764 or 662-627-7337 or visit ***www.clarksdaletourism.com.***

Look closely at the photo on the next page and you will learn much about traditions carried into the South by slaves imported from the Caribbean. The broken mirror by the door and the "bottle tree" with blue glass both contribute to warding off evil spirits. Look for the color blue, perhaps on the inner ceiling of the gallery (porch) or on the walls. It served the same purpose as the blue glass bottles. Normally the windows will be wide open (no air conditioning in the quarters!) and a veil of curtain will be blowing from the window. This, too, serves to scare off spirits (and perhaps disease-causing insects!).

Shack Up Inn

At the Hopson Plantation south of Clarksdale on Hwy. 49. Call 662-624-8329 for reservations.

This was an enjoyable B&B option. It's usually fully booked, so contact them early for reservations. Here B&B stands for "bed and beer" so don't look for breakfast! Although the individual "quarters" look very authentic on the outside, don't be fooled—they are modern and air conditioned inside!

"Shack" accommodations at Shack Up Inn. (Notice air conditioner in side wall—these aren't as primitive as they look.)

A BRIEF HISTORY OF BOLIVAR COUNTY[3]

Bolivar County was created in 1836 and named for General Simón Bolivar from South America. Inland towns in the Delta were slow to develop due to the difficulty of building roads. Railroads provided the first reliable transportation in the eastern part of the county. Today, county administration is split between Rosedale on the Mississippi

A Brief History of Cotton

Cotton has been used by humans to produce fabric for more than 4,500 years. The present U.S. "cotton belt" contained no cotton when early settlers arrived. They were familiar with cotton, however, and procured seed for planting. Numerous genetic stocks were tried, with the most successfully adapted crop resulting from Central American and Mexican plants. With the Industrial Revolution in the eighteenth century and the introduction of the cotton gin invented by Eli Whitney in 1793, cotton—white gold— became a major world and U.S. crop. It remains a major product of Mississippi and Arkansas.[4]

The pioneer planters in the Delta Region were often the wealthy younger sons of plantation owners to the east—in the Carolinas, Virginia, Georgia, etc. Land in the Delta was inexpensive, and the lumber covering it was valuable. Slave labor was readily transportable. Mass clear-cutting and draining of the Delta lowlands occurred in the nineteenth century with the help of slave labor at a time when human muscle was the primary agricultural machine. By the 1860s, slaves outnumbered whites in many Arkansas counties.

The hot, damp climate of the Delta was ideal for growing cotton. However, cotton needs constant weeding in order to thrive, contributing to the need for slave labor at a time when agricultural machinery was nonexistent. The white cotton bolls were picked and dropped into long canvas sacks that could hold hundreds of pounds of cotton. The bolls were embedded with tiny black seeds that had to be picked out by hand.

After the Civil War, financial depression and lack of labor prompted planters to diversify into soybeans, cattle, and grain. The scourge of the boll weevil in the 1920s brought an end to the era of "King Cotton."

River and Cleveland along the rail line, indicative of the importance of railroads to development of inland towns.

The first American settlement in Bolivar County was Georgetown, a landing on the river. In the 1850s, wealthy southern planters from the Carolinas, Virginia, Kentucky, Tennessee, Georgia, and Alabama were attracted to the area and used slaves to clear forest and swampland to develop plantations in the Yazoo Delta, deep in the heart of the South. It seemed that neither railroads nor abolitionist ideas had yet penetrated to disturb their empires.

**From Clarksdale, return to Hwy. 1 on Hwy. 322
and continue south to Rosedale**

Rosedale
Mile 585

Cotton gins along the highway occasionally allow visitors to look at the process of ginning cotton. Rosedale also plays a significant role in the Delta blues music culture

Great River Road State Park

In Rosedale off Hwy. 1. Food is available at the visitor center, and we recommend the catfish!

We very much enjoyed the opportunity to walk out on the sandbar at this 800-acre park. This vast sandbar grew as the river nibbled away at Napoleon and other towns on the opposite bank where the White and Arkansas rivers enter the Mississippi River from Arkansas.

Unfortunately, river bends tend to move south on the lower river, so between the sandbars and the migration of the bend, Rosedale today lies several miles from the river. In addition to our hike on the Dike Trail at Great River State Park, we enjoyed its 75-foot overlook.

At River mile 584 the Arkansas River enters the Mississippi on the opposite shore. Drive 30 miles south on Hwy. 1 to Greenville. The site of Mound Landing is along the way.

Mound Landing

River mile 560, 18 miles north of Greenville.

The **Mound Crevasse** is considered to be the first levee failure in the flood of 1927. Eventually the loss of life and property extended through seven states. On April 20, flood fighters noted seepage at the Mound Landing levee, and early on April 21, observers noted a large stream of water pouring through the earthen embankment. A violent "blowout" followed and within a few hours, the gap reached a width of 1,000 feet and growing.

In Greenville, flood fighters watched anxiously until it became clear that the municipal levee there would not hold. Floodwaters eventually flowed several feet deep on some of Greenville's streets, and many residents were eventually plucked from area mounds, rooftops, trees, levees, and other high spots.

Sand boils are one of the challenges faced by flood fighters on the levees. A sand boil is created when flood water seeps under the base of a levee through sand in the levee foundation. If the sand within erodes out through the top of the levee, the levee can collapse. Sand boils are usually brought under control by ringing them with sandbags to a height that equalizes the pressure and reduces the flow of water through them. During the flood of 1929, one sandboil about 15 feet wide across the top was reported, but it was controlled and the levee held.

NOTES

1 *The Southern Historical News, Inc.*, December 2002.

2 Plaque at the Fitzgerald Casino.

3 *The Southern Historical News, Inc.*, December 2002.

4 Information provided by the Bayer Corporation Research Station, Benoit, Mississippi.

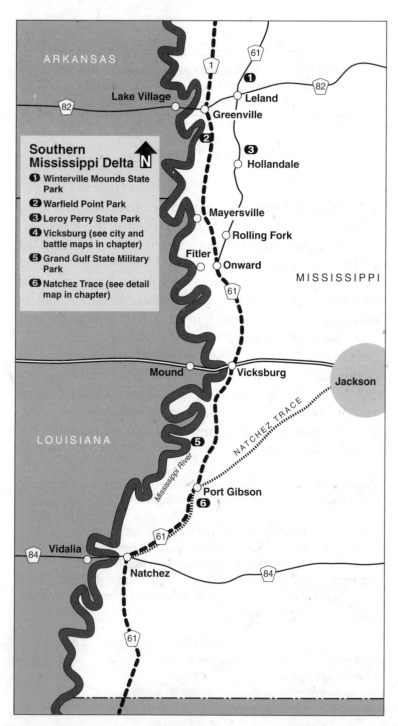

Southern Mississippi Delta N

❶ Winterville Mounds State Park
❷ Warfield Point Park
❸ Leroy Perry State Park
❹ Vicksburg (see city and battle maps in chapter)
❺ Grand Gulf State Military Park
❻ Natchez Trace (see detail map in chapter)

ARKANSAS

Lake Village

Leland

Greenville

Hollandale

Mayersville

Rolling Fork

Fitler

Onward

MISSISSIPPI

Mound

Vicksburg

Jackson

NATCHEZ TRACE

LOUISIANA

Mississippi River

Port Gibson

Vidalia

Natchez

4

Southern Mississippi Delta

Winterville Mounds State Park 🚶🚶⚑

Three miles north of Greenville on Hwy. 1. Informative interpretive museum with a small entrance fee. Walking trails. Closed Monday and Tuesday.

Winterville protects fifteen ceremonial earthen structures (all near Highway 1) built between AD 1200 and 1350. The site consisted originally of 23 mounds constructed around a 43-acre plaza, at the center of which is a 55-foot high temple mound. It appears from the lack of village remains that this was mostly a ceremonial site occupied by priests and chiefs rather than a village site. This site was likely abandoned in about 1400. This mound group is one of the largest and best-preserved in the southeastern United States and has been designated a National Historic Landmark. We were able to walk among the mounds and to grind corn with a stone mortar in the interpretive center. Mississippian artifacts here were among the best I've seen in museums along the river.

The Mississippian Mound Builders[1]

All of the publicly accessible mounds along the Mississippi River (Winterville, Emerald, and Grand Village) date from the Mississippian cultural division (AD 1000 to 1500). The mounds from this period mark centers of social and political authority for a vast, complex culture that had its center at Cahokia Mounds in Illinois just east of St. Louis, and stretched from Wisconsin south along the rivers.

Most of the Mississippian mounds are rectangular, flat-topped earthen platforms upon which temples or residences of chiefs and priests were erected. The great platform mounds range in height from 8 to almost 60 feet and are from 60 to 770 feet in width at the base. Building such structures required an advanced degree of social organization. Most likely the mounds were added to over the course of hundreds of years; the Indians carrying dirt and clay dug with shells and stone tools in woven baskets. There are often several layers representing succeeding eras of civilization in a single mound.

Greenville

Mile 537.2, Left bank descending

Greenville has had its struggles with the great river. The old city of Greenville perched precariously upriver along Bachelor Bend in the early nineteenth century until the river began eating it away and the town packed up and moved to its present, *somewhat* more secure location. As a river port, it became a target during the Civil War and was burned by the Union in May of 1863. The townsfolk persisted, however—to rebuild the town, fight off the river, cope with periodic yellow fever, and ultimately to survive the cutoff that took its river away altogether. Today, Greenville is the most populous town along the state of Mississippi's Great River Road.

INSIGHT

The Greenville Bends[2]

While the lower river is constantly reforming itself in a regular hunt for shortcuts to the sea, the USACE has made a place for itself by hurrying the process along. The USACE sketch below shows the three "cutoffs" that removed the "Greenville Bends" from the main channel of the Mississippi.

Promoting cutoffs has not always been a Corps policy. From 1892 through 1930, Corps policy was to protect bends by applying revetments, dikes, levees, etc., to hold the land. In the 1930s, after the flood of 1927, the Corps initiated its artificial cutoff program and the troublesome Greenville Bends were included.

The Ashbrook cutoff shortened the river by 13 miles. The Leland Cut was a natural cutoff that occurred in 1933 below Greenville, leaving that town nearly separated from the river. The USACE restored Greenville's status as a river town when it completed the Greenville Harbor Project in 1963. The old oxbow lake, renamed Lake Ferguson, now serves as a busy port for petroleum and agricultural chemicals, wood and paper products, and construction materials. Pleasure boaters will find fuel and supplies at the Greenville Harbor, River mile 537.2. The center of town is less than two blocks away.

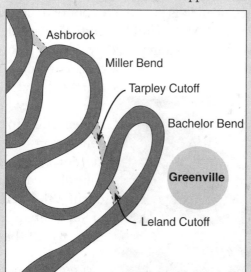

Straightening the Greenville Bends.

Weatherbee House

503 Washington Avenue, open Monday through Friday.
   This National Register of Historic Places home features rotating exhibits by local, regional, and national artists.

Waterfront Area

   Main and Central streets, just over the levee on Lake Ferguson. Walk a levee that is taller and longer than the Great Wall of China! Greenville's two casinos, the Bayou Caddy Jubilee and Lighthouse Point, are both located here. Several modern chain hotels are located in the immediate area.

Delta Blues Festival

Third Saturday in September. Ethnic foods, arts and crafts. For information, call 662-334-2711.

McCormick Book Inn

825 Main St.
   Enjoy a wealth of regional books as well as a fine collection of first edition books, historic photos, and memorabilia on display toward the back of the store.
   Owner Hugh McCormick is passionate about Greenville and southern literature. McCormick credits Greenville's literary wealth (William Alexander Percy, Shelby Foote, Bern Keating, Walker Percy, Ellen Douglas, and Hodding Carter all lived in the vicinity of Greenville) to a generation of excellent public school teachers during the reign of Superintendent E.E. Bass. (Bass

McCormick Book Inn.

introduced the concept of allowing students to reuse textbooks rather than having to purchase them each year. It was an unusual concept then because people didn't know how diseases spread—and one possible source was believed to be textbooks.) Besides the schools having great teachers, general interest in literacy was so strong in the 1920s and '30s that even cigarette packages offered tiny free books. In short, McCormick summarized, it was a literary time, the residents were well educated by the public school system, and they had living examples in Percy and Cohn to relate to.

Warfield Point Park

Inside the levee about 2 miles south of Greenville on Hwy. 82 west. Observation tower, boat ramp, picnic and camping areas. Call 662-335-7275 for information or reservations.

This large U.S. Army Corps of Engineers park is the only riverside campground between St. Louis and New Orleans.

The levee drive to Warfield Point Park offers opportunities to see birds and wildlife in the burrow pits alongside the road. While the old towboat in the park is in disrepair, it is worth a good look, as it was powered solely by paddlewheel.

The sandbar at Warfield Point is closed to the public. Like many sandbars on the lower river, it can be treacherous. While sandbars on the upper river are normally quite

Old sternwheel towboat naer Warfield Point Park.

safe, the meandering nature of the river on the lower river should make nearly every sandbar suspect to the visitor.

Continue south on Hwy. 1 and 61 toward Vicksburg (80 miles). Or cross the bridge back to Lake Village, Arkansas, to visit Lake Village State Park before continuing south in Mississippi (recommended, see page 36).

Leroy Percy State Park

Hollandale, Hwy. 12. 662-827-5436. Restaurant, cabins, fishing, camping, nature trail, meeting rooms.

This, the largest and oldest of Mississippi's state parks, is characterized by bubbling hot springs, cypress trees, and ancient live oaks dripping with Spanish moss. It features a wildlife preserve with a boardwalk through alligator habitat.

Continue south on Hwy. 1 to Mayersville.
If time is short, jump onto Hwy. 14 at Mayersville and return to Hwy. 61 to Rolling Fork and on to Onward. If river levels and time permit once you reach Onward, wander down Hwy. 1 to Fitler.
Old Hwy. 61 is known as Mississippi's "Blues Highway" because it was the route many Delta blues musicians followed to the North in the hunt for jobs. BB King, Little Richard, and Muddy Waters are just a few of the local legends who went on to international stardom

DISTANCES FROM GREENVILLE TO:

Memphis	146 miles
Little Rock	164 miles
Nashville	363 miles
New Orleans	294 miles
Atlanta	428 miles
Dallas	393 miles

INSIGHT

Spanish Moss[3]

Spanish moss is a picturesque plant that first appears along the river near Greenville. In fact, the Arkansas border was basically set at the northernmost point where Spanish moss can thrive. While it cannot live without the support of other plants, it is *not* a parasite. It does not receive any nourishment from its host and does not damage the tree on which it hangs. It is a green plant with tiny gray scales that trap the dust and water that nourish it. Plants are categorized by flower structure rather than leaf, seed, or fruit structure, so oddly enough, the seldom-noticed flower of Spanish moss reveals that it is most closely related to the pineapple!

Cajuns and others who lived along the bayous and wetlands of Louisiana once harvested the plant, dried it, and sold it to the Ford Motor Company, which used it to stuff car seats. It was also used to stuff mattresses, furniture, and more.

Kudzu covers everything along the river road in Mississippi, but is especially abundant in the frequently flooded stretch of river delta from Greenville to Vicksburg. The thick green vine was originally introduced to protect farmland from erosion. It grows an average of six inches per day, swallowing up derelict machinery, telephone poles, even trees and buildings.

Mayersville
Mile 496.5 AHP

This small town is the county seat for sparsely populated Issaquena County. On the riverfront are an oil terminal and a grain elevator.

Rolling Fork

The birthplace of blues great Muddy Waters is located where Hwy. 1 intersects with Hwy 61 at Rolling Fork.

Onward
Hwy. 61

The Onward Store displays photos of President Theodore Roosevelt's famous bear hunt and offers souvenir teddy bears for sale.[4]

Fitler
Hwy. 1

Fitler had developed around the Fitler Plantation landing by 1900. It boasted electric lights, stores, warehouses, a big steam cotton gin, and a bakery. But steamboats were already on the way out, and the remains of the town have disappeared (though the name is still on the map!).

INSIGHT

Roosevelt's Teddy Bear

We were surprised to see a yellow "Bear Crossing" sign just outside of Greenville. Apparently southern bears (as well as alligators, waterfowl, and other wildlife) inhabit the bayous and "burrow pits" beside the levees. We were told that as many as sixty brown bears may inhabit one of the large river islands near Greenville. When water levels drop, the bears swim across the river to visit the catfish farms and could conceivably be seen lounging in a cotton field.

It was this southern brown bear that made the *teddy bear* a popular stuffed animal. The story is that in 1902 Teddy Roosevelt came to the area to hunt bear. His hunting guide, the legendary Holt Collier of Greenville, promised Roosevelt would get a bear, even if Collier had to tie one to a tree. Collier was as good as his word. In fact, he captured a bear, and when the bear attacked his prize dog, Collier beat it with his rifle butt and tied it to a tree for Roosevelt to shoot. When Roosevelt refused to shoot the helpless bear, the story of Teddy's bear hit the papers nationwide. A New York resident conceived the idea of a loveable, soft "Teddy Bear" and the Ideal Toy Company was born.

Albemarle Lake, south of Fitler, was a deep 14-mile bend in the river until 1913, when the river suddenly abandoned its old Albemarle Bend and developed the Newman Cutoff. Likewise, the oxbow Eagle Lake was once Eagle Bend. Here, the swamps and baldcypress forests made an excellent habitat for the American bald eagle. Now the swamps have been drained, the cypress cleared. The USACE has built a new structure that will artificially provide protection and fresh water to the old oxbow.

A BRIEF HISTORY OF WARREN COUNTY

Jean Baptiste LeMoyne, Sieur de Bienville[5] established his Fort St. Pierre on the bluff where Vicksburg now sits in 1715 only to see it wiped out by hostile Indians. Spain seized the Natchez district in 1781 and claimed the Yazoo River as the northern boundary of Spanish West Florida. While the American and Spanish governments debated the issue, the Spanish commandant of the Natchez district set out with a detachment of soldiers and began the construction of a military post called Fort Nogales, *nogales* being Spanish for "walnuts."

Just before the American Revolution, many British subjects loyal to England requested permission from Spain to settle in the area of modern-day Vicksburg to avoid the conflict on the East Coast. But settlers were required to accept Roman Catholicism, something many could never do—and so they never really became assimilated into the Spanish culture.

In March of 1798, the Spanish agreed to abandon their Fort to the Americans. The American garrison moved in and renamed it Fort McHenry, and the American settlers followed immediately behind.

Vicksburg

River mile 437.1.
Population 26,200

A BRIEF HISTORY OF THE CITY OF VICKSBURG

The main city of Vicksburg (also known as Fort St. Pierre by the French in 1715; Fort Nogales by the Spanish in 1719; and Fort McHenry by the Americans) was settled in 1811 by a Methodist minister, the Reverend Newit Vick, when the Spanish ceded the site to the American garrison. Vick seized the opportunity to buy a bluffland claim of 1,100 acres from a restless farmer and sat down with a piece of paper to plan his town. He sold two lots before he and his wife died on the same day, victims of fever. The land and the dream were left to his thirteen children.

The public auction of lots in the town was a big success. The town grew rapidly as doctors came to fight epi-
demics of yellow fever, smallpox, and cholera. Lawyers
gathered to argue claims under British, Spanish, and American land grants. It was incorporated in 1825 and quickly
developed a disreputable levee district nearly as well-
known as was "Natchez under the hill." The advent of
steamboats, the invention of the cotton gin, and the
removal of the Indians provided energy for the new settlement. Vicksburg thrived as a shipping port for cotton.
Its population in 1860 was 4,600; a hundred years later,
Vicksburg numbered 42,206.

During the winter of 1863, Abraham Lincoln sent U.S.
Grant to take command of the campaign against Vicks-
burg, which in turn would give the North control of the
Lower Mississippi.

The soft loess that formed the bluffs of Vicksburg made
it possible to dig caves, which protected the citizens from
daily Union bombardments. The going rate for cave-diggers
was $35 to dig a one-room cave and $50 for two rooms.
The caves were damp and full of bugs, but they did save
lives. Vicksburg, you must remember, was being bom-
barded from the river a year before the siege began. During the siege, approximately 60,000 rounds a day were fired
upon the city. After the forty-seven-day siege, the city surrendered on July 4, 1863.

*Vicksburg cave exhibit
at Military Park.*

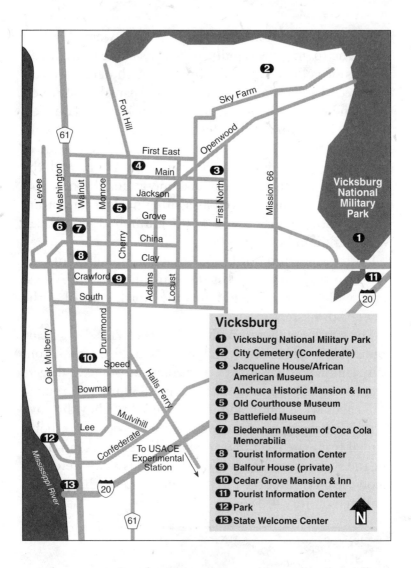

Vicksburg

1 Vicksburg National Military Park
2 City Cemetery (Confederate)
3 Jacqueline House/African American Museum
4 Anchuca Historic Mansion & Inn
5 Old Courthouse Museum
6 Battlefield Museum
7 Biedenharn Museum of Coca Cola Memorabilia
8 Tourist Information Center
9 Balfour House (private)
10 Cedar Grove Mansion & Inn
11 Tourist Information Center
12 Park
13 State Welcome Center

Like many Southerners we met, Betty, our guide at Vicksburg National Military Park, had a positive view of the Northern general, Ulysses S. Grant. He was generous in his terms of surrender, and the Union soldiers were generous about providing food from their own knapsacks to the citizens. At the end of the siege, campfires dotted the city—not from looting, but from Union soldiers cooking up whatever they had to feed the starving locals and Confederate soldiers. When Grant died, he requested that an equal number of Union and Confederate generals serve as his pallbearers. President Grover S. Cleveland invited Grant's wife to choose two of each.

Although the USACE opened the Yazoo Diversion Canal in 1903, steamboats would never again visit Vicksburg in any number. It would be 100 years before the town again celebrated the Fourth of July.

WHAT TO SEE IN VICKSBURG

Washington Street is the main thoroughfare in Vicksburg. Speed Street commemorates the Union officer who overloaded the *Sultana*. Note that stoplights for each intersection are numbered to make it easier for locals to direct visitors. This concept was originally introduced by the Tourism Bureau, but it makes giving directions so much easier that now the locals use the numbering system as well.

1858 Old Courthouse

1008 Cherry Street.

This beautiful courthouse was spared during the Civil War only because Union prisoners were held in the upper story. The museum has a large collection of city artifacts. During our December visit, at the annual Confederate Christmas Ball, participants in full 1860s dress reenacted an attack by the Union that had during the traditional Vicksburg Christmas Ball.

The Old Courthouse.

Vicksburg Battlefield Museum

4137 I-20 Frontage Rd., is located at the Battlefield Inn near the Vicksburg National Military Park.

This private museum boasts the world's largest collection of Civil War gunboat models and numerous artifacts relating to the battles near Vicksburg. The owners, who developed the museum and continue to build their models there, are passionate about their subject. A multimedia presentation, *Vanishing Glory*, which tells the story of the siege of Vicksburg, is shown at the museum on the hour.

Biedenharn Museum of Coca-Cola History

1107 Washington Street.

It was here that a young merchant by the name of Joseph Biedenharn first bottled Coca-Cola for shipping to rural areas. An authentically restored 1890s candy store and soda fountain are on the site. We thoroughly enjoyed the Attic Art Gallery nearby, especially works by regional artist Kenneth Humphrey.

Riverboat Casinos

Four casinos are located in riverboats along the Vicksburg waterfront.

Riverside Park

This park is the only public assess to the river. During the flood of 1927, the river at this point was 72 miles wide! The river might have risen as high as Pearl Street during floods before the construction of levees after the flood of 1927.

Anchuca Bed & Breakfast

1010 First East Street. For information or reservations, call 888-686-0111.

Anchuca ("happy home" in Choctaw) is an 1830 Greek Revival mansion built by an ice and coal merchant. Jefferson Davis once addressed the townspeople from the

---

INSIGHT

Antebellum Homes
(ante = before; bellum = war)

Most of the better homes in Vicksburg originally belonged to the merchant class. True millionaires from the Planter Society were clustered farther south, from Natchez to Baton Rouge. It is believed that there were more millionaires along that stretch of the Lower Mississippi than anywhere else in the United States.

Even in Natchez, however, society was dominated by merchants after the Civil War. Businessmen from the North came south in the winter, cleared the forests for timber, and invested the proceeds in cotton. Other merchants made their fortunes by fueling the switch from wood-burning to coal-burning heat and the switch to electricity.

Many of the merchants' great homes were built with lumber purchased from rafters—boatmen who floated goods down from the North before the advent of the steamboat. Upon selling their goods, the rafters broke up their crafts and sold the logs for lumber. The crews then most likely returned north on foot via the Natchez Trace.

A dozen historic antebellum homes are open for tours in Vicksburg.

---

home's balcony. We had a delightful B&B experience there; we stayed in the slave quarters, which have rough tile floors and fireplaces. The collected furnishings of Anchuca make it a virtual museum.

Balfour House

Crawford Street and Cherry.

This house dates from 1835 and is considered to be one of the state's finest Greek revival structures. It is next door to the home of General John Clifford Pemberton, a Southern general during the Battle of Vicksburg. Balfour House will soon be open to the public as an adjunct to the National Military Park.

Cedar Grove Estate Restaurant & Inn ⚑

2300 Washington. Phone 800-862-1300 for reservations. There are 20 luxurious guest rooms, and the home is open daily for tours.

We had a delicious dinner here, too! The restored mansion is beautifully furnished and has four acres of gardens, courtyards, fountains and gazebos.

Walnut Hills Round Table Restaurant

1214 Adams St.

We enjoyed a bountiful Sunday dinner at a round table here. Dinners are served family style with a huge "lazy Susan" at each table. There was pecan pie, of course, but also hush puppies, greens, fried chicken, and much more!

You'll enjoy a "round" meal at Walnut Hills.

Vicksburg National Military Park ⚑

1800 acres. The Vicksburg National Military Cemetery, with 17,000 Union soldiers. USS Cairo, a Union ironclad gunboat, now a museum. Extensive Visitor Center (601-636-0583) with exhibits and artifacts from the siege of Vicksburg. 16-mile driving tour through the well-preserved battlefields.

We were blessed to have Betty England as our park guide, and we have added her to our collected memories of people who were truly passionate about their subject. Betty should have long since retired from the workaday world, yet her enthusiasm, storehouse of stories, and knowledge made our Vicksburg visit memorable!

There are 1,348 monuments in the park; some are regimental monuments, some are elaborate state monuments, some are small square stones that mark the positions of army sharpshooters. Generally, the veteran groups involved in the battles were allowed to choose the location of their monument. It will not be possible for you to stop and read all the monuments in a single visit! The best plan is note in advance the state monuments you most want to visit.

According to Betty, each monument is unique to the regiment or state it represents. For example, the Wisconsin monument is made of Wausau granite, and Old Abe the eagle sits watchfully above the entire monument. A winter wind blows away the soldier's brass coat, and a cavalryman leads his horse on foot, as the bluffs were too steep to fight on horseback. While such winter clothing would not have been necessary in Mississippi, it reflects that it was the coldest winter on record. Minnesota chose an exceptionally large obelisk to commemorate the fact that it sent a number of soldiers far out of proportion to its population.

Missouri's monument reflects that it had soldiers on both sides of the war. At night, a *trysting line* was established for the Missourians so that friends and relatives who fought one another during the day could visit during the night. Because of the siege, the Confederates could not get mail or family news in and out, so the Northern Missouri soldiers would bring their letters to the trysting line and share their news with Confederate soldiers hungry for news from home.

Old Abe sits atop the Wisconsin monument.

The Story of Albert D. J. Cashier

One of Betty's more interesting stories was of the 95th Illinois Regiment. This regiment had a reputation as a particularly fierce group of fighters. It had been through the Battle of Shiloh, where 42 percent of the regiment had been lost. Among those at Vicksburg was one they called "the fiercest of the fierce"—Albert D. J. Cashier.

In 1913 Albert was severely injured in a car accident. A doctor arrived on the scene, but Albert refused to allow the doctor to help him unless the doctor promised not to reveal his secret—that Albert was a woman. Inevitably, Albert's secret leaked out and a movement began in Illinois to have his name stricken from the Vicksburg monument, a fairly common practice for someone who lost the approval of another member of the regiment. But in 1915, representatives of the regiment met in Chicago and signed a communication to the Illinois governor requesting that if any one name were stricken from the regimental listing, then *every* name must be taken off. Albert's name is still listed to this day.

Betty's personal theory is that "Albert" was once engaged to a man named Albert in Ireland. When he was killed in an uprising, she committed herself to carrying on his life by following through on their dream to come to the United States. She dressed as a man, stowed away on a ship, and enrolled in the war using Albert's name. According to Betty, at least 600 women are documented to have fought in the Civil War as men.

Albert Cashier is the "man" on the right.

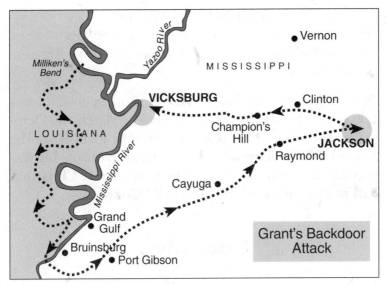

The Battle of Vicksburg.

Seventy-seven thousand Union soldiers and 19,000 Confederates participated in this battle. Seventy-five percent of those who signed up for the war from Mississippi were either killed or wounded. In fact, after the war, fully 47 percent of all men in Mississippi were amputees, and the state spent 20 percent of its budget for three years to pay for their artificial limbs. Iowa had 26,000 males, and 13,001 signed up to fight. Seventeen thousand Northern soldiers (nearly 12,000 unknown) are buried at the Vicksburg National Military Cemetery. Southern soldiers are buried separately. Having fought against their country, they were no longer considered American citizens and were not allowed government burials.

U.S.S. *Cairo* Museum

Visit this museum just as you exit the Union line in the Military Park. Do not leave the park at this point, as you will miss the Confederate battle lines. The *Cairo* is an ironclad Union gunboat that was sunk during the war and raised from the Yazoo River one hundred years afterward (1965).

VICKSBURG EVENTS

Phone 800-221-3536 for more information on any of these events, including RiverFest in mid-April and the Civil War reenactment in May.

Many of the mansions in Vicksburg offer public tours—**"pilgrimages"**—for a small fee in March and October of each year. In July a reenactment focuses on the **Assault at Vicksburg,** with demonstrations of how life was for citizens during the siege. The **Confederate Christmas Ball** in December is held at the Old Courthouse.

Yazoo River
River mile 437.1.

This tributary of the Lower Mississippi originally entered the river several miles above Vicksburg. In 1699, Tunica Indians occupied villages along the banks of the Yazoo, and Father Antoine Davion, a French priest, established a mission among them. The French fort there was attacked and destroyed in 1729, and the French deserted the Yazoo River valley. Choctaw Indians subsequently inhabited the area until their removal in the 1830s.

During the Civil War, Confederate forces sank many of their boats in the Yazoo to prevent their capture by the Union forces. The Union gunboat *Cairo* remained buried in the mud of the river until resurrected in 1965.

Davis Island
Palmyra Lake at River mile 415.5. ⚓

A sign along Highway 61 points in the direction of Davis Island (now privately owned), which once was home to **Brierfield** and **Hurricane**, plantations belonging to Joseph and Jefferson Davis. Davis Island was a peninsula at the time, and the bend in the river was known as Davis Bend. During the Battle of Vicksburg, the two plantations were confiscated and turned over to the Freedman's Bureau to become a model colony of ex-slaves. The colony was never successful.

After the war, Joseph Davis regained possession of the land by signing an oath of loyalty to the Union. Jefferson Davis, so briefly the president of the Confederacy, was placed in solitary confinement for two years after the war. He refused to take the loyalty oath, saying that it was his sincere belief that any state had the right to secede. When a recent U.S. Congress offered to grant citizenship to Jefferson Davis posthumously, it was declined by his great-grandson. He felt that since Davis had refused to accept it during his lifetime, it would be inappropriate to accept it after his death.

Two years after the war ended, a natural cutoff occurred and Davis Bend, previously a peninsula, became Davis Island. The oxbow lake that was once Davis Bend is now called Palmyra Lake. The descendants of the Davis slaves are said to have lived on the island well into the 1930s.

Continue south on Hwy. 61 for 20 miles and then west on Grand Gulf Road (8 Miles) to Grand Gulf Military Park (not to be missed) in Claiborne County.

Claiborne and Jefferson Counties

The Choctaw Indian nation, rivals of the Chickasaw farther north, occupied 26 villages in present-day Claiborne County. It was a region rich with the resources of the Mississippi and the Black Rivers. The first European settlement was established in 1729 as a hunting village near Petit Gulf, just north of Rodney. The county was formed in 1775 and was named for W. C. Claiborne, governor of the territory. The settlement of Port Gibson began when Samuel Gibson acquired 820 acres from the Spanish. A settlement that had grown up at Gibson's Landing by 1788 was incorporated as Port Gibson in 1811. The Choctaw relinquished their right to the land with the signing of the Treaty of Commissioner's Creek in 1802. The Choctaw still live in Mississippi at a reservation near Philadelphia in east central Mississippi.

Charles Cole Claiborne was 26 years old when President Thomas Jefferson appointed him governor of the Mississippi Territory. In 1803, he and James Wilkinson were chosen to take possession of the vast Louisiana Territory. He eventually became governor of the Orleans Territory and was elected senator in 1817. He died that year at the age of 42.

When General Grant made Port Gibson the first objective in his campaign to take Vicksburg, the county took on great strategic importance in the Civil War. The fortifications are preserved at Grand Gulf State Park.

Grand Gulf
River mile 407.

Grand Gulf was a major river port until the Mississippi flooded the entire downtown area in the 1850s. By the time of the Civil War, there were only 150 residents. The name refers to a vicious eddy that threatened flatboats and canoes at the foot of the bluff. Today what remains of the town is located well away from the riverfront. A high metal marker at the boat launch near the state park museum provides a graphic reminder of how dramatically river stages can change. In the flood of 1973, the river stage was 56.3 feet. In 1937 it was 53 feet, in 1929, 52 feet.

While you view the main river channel at this point, notice that buoys mark the main channel. The red "nuns" have pointed tops, and the green "cans" have flat tops, so that even if the colors don't show clearly, river pilots are able to identify the type of can. The rule of the river is *red right return—red* nuns to the *right* of the boat when *returning* home from the sea (or traveling upriver).

The Grand Gulf Nuclear Station is barely visible along the road to the Military Park. This 1,300-megawatt boiling water reactor is the largest of its type in the country.

Grand Gulf State Military Park

Grand Gulf preserves 400 acres of Confederate fortifications. There is an observation tower for viewing the river. A state-operated RV park within the park offers 42 sites with electricity, water and sewage. $15/night or $12 if over 60 years.

This park offers an excellent local museum with such unique items as a very rare Civil War ambulance made by Studebaker and an early submarine used to run liquor from Davis Island to the Louisiana shore early in the prohibition period. The propellers were powered by a Model-T Ford engine. The eclectic museum also contains an excellent fossil display including shells, shark teeth and a mammoth tooth—all collected locally.

Grand Gulf was an important Confederate stronghold because of its riverside location. On April 29, 1863, Union ironclads *Louisville*, *Pittsburg*, *Carondelet*, *Tuscumbia*, *Lafayette*, *Mound City*, and Admiral Porter's *Benton* began pouring thousands of rounds of

Flood level marker near the state park museum.

83

ammunition upon the village, but rebel guns were not silenced. After the defeat of Port Gibson, the Confederates deserted the site and U.S. Grant occupied it, planning to use it as a supply base for his attack on Vicksburg. Instead, he decided to leave the supply base behind and take his army through the interior, approaching Vicksburg from the rear.

On April 30, 40,000 Union soldiers landed at the Bruinsburg landing—the largest amphibious landing by the United States until World War II. For 30 days, the army fought its way via Raymond, Jackson, Champions Hill and the Big Black River to the rear of Vicksburg, where they began the siege against that city.

Bruinsburg began as a landing for the plantation of Bryan Bruin and his son, Peter. The Bruins arrived in June 1788 with a party of 80 people from Virginia. Each family was promised 680 acres by the Spanish governor, and the Bruins established their plantation on Bayou Pierre (Stone). Bryan Bruin later became one of the first territorial judges for the U.S. government. The Bruins' home became a popular stop for distinguished visitors, including Aaron Burr in 1807.

It was widely believed that Aaron Burr was involved in a mysterious plot to seize New Orleans and attack Mex-

Submarine at Grand Gulf State Military Park.

ico. Burr told the Bruins that he was planning to establish a settlement on some land he had purchased in the Ouachita River Basin of Louisiana. When he learned that the U.S. militia had been called out and that eight armed gunboats had been sent from New Orleans to intercept him, he promptly gave himself up to authorities, eventually to be tried and acquitted of charges of treason.

Follow Hwy. 61 south from Vicksburg to Port Gibson and the Natchez Trace Parkway.

Ashland Landing
Mile 381, left bank descending. ⚓

General Zachary Taylor, elected president in 1848, owned a plantation in this vicinity.

Giles Cutoff
Mile 367, left bank descending. ⚓

Lake Concordia in Louisiana, just above Giles Bend, may be where Hernando de Soto's body was weighted and deposited after his death near present-day Ferriday, Louisiana. Of course Lake Village likes to make the same claim!

Natchez Trace Parkway

Just south of Port Gibson, the Natchez Trace Parkway provides a scenic tree-lined route to Natchez. The parkway has been designated a National Scenic Byway and extends for 400 miles—from Natchez to Nashville, Tennessee—and includes several interpretive displays. No commercial traffic is allowed on the parkway.

A Brief History of the Natchez Trace

The Trace (or path) most likely evolved as native Natchez, Choctaw, and Chickasaw Indians followed the traditional hunting trails already "traced" by their ancestors. When Spanish and French explorers entered the area, they, too, followed the narrow trails, beating them down and widening them nearly into roads. The Trace appears on French maps as early as 1733 as "The Path to the Choctaw Nation," running from Natchez to salt licks in Central Tennessee.

As Americans settled the Ohio River Valley, farmers who shipped goods downriver in flatboats sold not only their goods, but also the lumber from their boats. They then returned on foot, following the Natchez Trace to the northeast. By 1820, thirty "stands"—primitive inns—provided basic food and shelter along the trail. The Mount Locust Inn along the Natchez Trace Parkway is a restored example of such an inn.

Though the Trace was one of the busiest highways in the country from 1800 to 1820, it was neither safe nor comfortable. Bandits, flooding, and disease were ever-present dangers. Travel on the Trace was happily avoided once steamboats made it possible to travel upriver in relative comfort and safety.

Farmers shipped their goods downriver and returned home on foot.

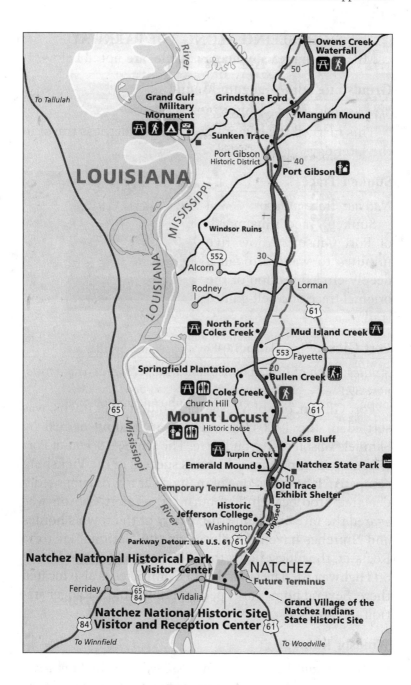

SIGHTSEEING ALONG THE PARKWAY

Milepost markers, when available, are noted below.[6]

Grindstone Ford/Mangum Mound

Natchez Trace milepost 45.7.

This marked the beginning of true wilderness travel in the later days of the Trace.

Sunken Trace

Natchez Trace milepost 41.5.

Sunken Trace is just north of Port Gibson. Allow five minutes to walk through a deeply eroded section of the original trace on a self-guided trail.

Sunken Trace.

Port Gibson[7] (population 1,048)

8 miles south of Canemount Plantation, Natchez Trace milepost 39.2.

Port Gibson, one of Mississippi's oldest river towns, was settled in the 1700s around a boat landing owned by Samuel Gibson on Bayou Pierre. The Union's defeat of Port Gibson was important to Grant's success in the Vicksburg campaign. It was also one of many river towns supposedly declared "too beautiful to burn," thus Port Gibson was spared the fate of Grand Gulf. Many of the town's homes and churches have been placed on the National Historic Register, the oldest being the 1805 **Samuel Gibson House** on Highway 61. The Chamber of Commerce is also located there. Several homes are open for public tours. Ranger station on site.

Windsor Ruins

On Canemount Plantation, Hwy. 552 west, about 12 miles.

Canemount itself is no longer open to the public. Here, Mississippi's most spectacular mansion escaped

Windsor ruins.

destruction by Union forces only to be destroyed in a fire in February of 1890.

Smith Coffe Daniell II, a successful cotton planter, completed construction of Windsor in 1861. Daniell owned 21,000 acres of plantation land in Louisiana and Mississippi. A man in our tour group mentioned that one of the stories in his family (he was descended from slaves) was about women in this society sending their ball gowns back to Paris for cleaning. Many of the children were also sent back to Europe for schooling and socializing.

Daniell died in April of 1861, only a few weeks after completing the mansion. His wife and children continued to live here but lost much of the family's holdings during the Civil War.

The basic style of Windsor was Greek revival with details borrowed from Italianate and Gothic architecture. The mansion had 23 rooms, an above-ground basement, two residential floors, and an attic. An L-shaped extension on the east side contained the kitchen, pantry and dining rooms. Rainwater stored in large cisterns supplied two bathrooms.

Reproduction of Windsor built in Texas in the 1990s.

All photographs and drawings of Windsor were thought to have been lost in the fire of 1890, but in 1991 historians discovered a sketch of it drawn by a Union soldier. (Mississippi Dept. of Archives and History.) The plans for the structure were also eventually discovered and an exact reproduction was rebuilt in Texas for $2million dollars. It has 35,000 square feet of living space!

Continue on Hwy. 552 as it loops back to Hwy. 61 and south to Lorman. Several other mansions are open to the public for tours and accommodations. Look for Rosswood, two miles east of Lorman on Hwy. 552.

North Fork Coles Creek   ⊼

Picnic area.

Mud Island Creek   ⊼

Picnic area.

Springfield Plantation   ⌐

Halfway between Fayette and the Natchez Trace Parkway. Daily tours. 601-786-3802.

Springfield, built between 1786 and 1791, has been a working plantation for over two hundred years. Andrew Jackson married Rachel Robards here.

Bullen Creek   🚶🚶

Natchez Trace milepost 18.4. A self-guiding trail leads through a mixed hardwood-pine forest. Allow 15 minutes.

Coles Creek   ⊼

Natchez Trace milepost 17.5. Picnic areas, restrooms.

Mount Locust Historic House   ⌐

Natchez Trace milepost 15.5. Restrooms, exhibits, bookstore and ranger station.

At this restored historic "stand," interpretive programs are offered from February through November.

Loess Bluff   ⌐

Natchez Trace milepost 12.4.

Deposits of topsoil were blown here during the Ice Age, when glaciers covered the northern half of the United States. The deposits settled on the gravel, sand, and clay ridges of an ancient sea bed. During this time, nearly continuous dust storms blew in from the west and covered the area with dust to a depth of 30 to 90 feet.

While loess originally covered a vast area, it is now restricted to a narrow band of hills 3 to 30 miles wide on the east bank of the Mississippi from Baton Rouge to Ten-

Loess bluff.

nessee. Where the Natchez Trace passed through loess, the roads eroded to as much as 20 feet deep (see photo above).

Turpin Creek

Natchez Trace milepost 12.1. Picnic area.

Emerald Mound

Natchez Trace milepost 10.3. About 10 miles northeast of Natchez. Exit the Parkway at the Rte 553 intersection and follow signs about 1 mile to the mound. A walking trail leads to the top.

Don't pass by this National Historic Landmark! Emerald Mound, measuring 770 by 435 feet at the base and 35 feet tall, covers 8 acres and is the second largest mound in the United States! Emerald Mound and several smaller mounds in the group were used as a ceremonial center between AD 1250 and 1400 by ancestors of the Natchez Indians. By the time de Soto passed through the area in 1540–41, the Natchez had already abandoned Emerald and established their capital at the Grand Village, 12 miles to the southwest.

Old Trace Exhibit Shelter

Natchez Trace milepost 8.7.
Stop here to see an old section of the original trace.

Historic Jefferson College ⚑

Natchez Trace milepost 8.8 in Washington.

The College was named for President Thomas Jefferson in 1802. Visitors can tour the beautiful buildings and grounds daily. Closed Sunday mornings. 601-442-2901.

The Parkway ends at its intersection with Highway 61, and the traveler is back in the four-lane world. The Natchez Trace Visitor Center is in Tupelo, Mississippi at Mile 266 (the midway point for the trail). The Natchez National Historical Park Headquarters is located in Natchez at Melrose. The Traceway Campground is located just outside the park on Highway 61. Continue south on Hwy 61 for 7 miles to Natchez.

Natchez

River mile 363.8.
Population 18,464.

WHAT TO SEE IN NATCHEZ

More than 600 opulent antebellum homes still stand in the Natchez area. For the traveler, Natchez is unique—its mansions are its primary draw. Many wealthy planters built their mansions in the immediate area of Natchez and then traveled to oversee their plantations along the river. No major battles occurred here as there were no railroads or other strategic military reasons for the enemy to hold it.

Some of the best known mansions are Longwood, Stanton Hall, Rosalie, Monmouth, Dunleith, and Magnolia Hall.

Many of the plantations along the Lower Mississippi host spring and fall "pilgrimages." Public tours enable tens of thousands of tourists each year to tour homes along the entire stretch of Great River Road, but most notably in Vicksburg and Natchez. For information on the spring and fall pilgrimages, call 800-647-6742.

The French and the Natchez

French brothers and explorers Pierre Le Moyne, Sieur d'Iberville, and Jean Baptiste Le Moyne, Sieur de Bienville, explored the Lower River in the early years of the seventeenth century. They discovered the Natchez Indians, intelligent and proud, on the bluffs near present-day Natchez. The Natchez are believed to represent the last gasp of the Mississippian Indian culture. Journals contemporary to Bienville record many of the rituals associated with the raised Mississippian mound settlements found throughout the Mississippi River Valley.

In 1716 the French constructed Fort Rosalie on the bluff. The Natchez and a few French settlers lived together peacefully enough until 1729, when the Natchez rose up to defeat the soldiers and killed most of the 200 settlers. While the military garrison was eventually strengthened, the Treaty of Paris brought an end to French expansion into the area.

In 1763, after the Treaty of Paris, Natchez became the property of Great Britain. Although the British did everything they could to encourage settlement, it wasn't until Spain seized the outpost that it began to flourish. In 1795, the United States signed a treaty with Spain that designated the east bank of the Mississippi as far south as the 31st parallel to be American Territory. It was 1798 before the Spanish garrison withdrew and Captain Isaac Guion was left in undisputed possession of the future town site. American settlers promptly made Natchez the most important settlement in the new Mississippi Territory.

During our visit, we stayed at the Winslow House, a simple B&B in old downtown Natchez. It made a comfortable staging point for walking tours of Natchez. Our second night was at Monmouth.

Longwood

Lower Woodville Road

Longwood is a magnificent octagonal shell begun in the late 1850s. It was left incomplete by northern tradesmen who vacated the site immediately upon the outbreak of Civil War. As the holdings of the family were destroyed during the war, they lived out the rest of their lives on the lower floor. It is the largest octagonal structure in the South, but it remains unfinished.

Longwood.

Monmouth Plantation ⚐

36 Melrose Ave.

Guest rooms offer the traveler a unique experience of old-world elegance. Grounds are extensive and beautifully landscaped. An elegant family-style dinner is served at 7:30 p.m. We enjoyed spinach salad, roasted red pepper/olive oil ragout, mustard-encrusted bone-in pork loin, and sweet potato souflée. Reservations are required. 800-828-4531.

Monmouth sitting room.

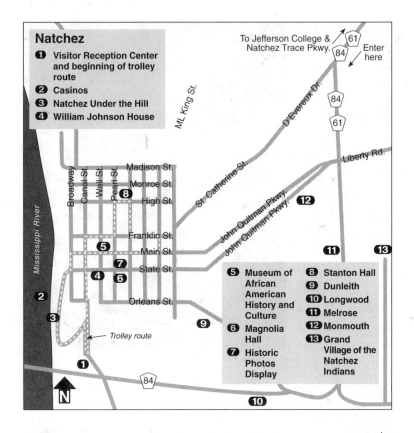

Natchez

1. Visitor Reception Center and beginning of trolley route
2. Casinos
3. Natchez Under the Hill
4. William Johnson House

To Jefferson College & Natchez Trace Pkwy.

Enter here

ML King St.

D'Evereux Dr.

Liberty Rd.

Mississippi River

Broadway
Canal St.
Wall St.
Pearl St.

Madison St.
Monroe St.
High St.

St. Catherine St.

Franklin St.
Main St.
State St.

Orleans St.

John Quitman Pkwy.
John Quitman Pkwy.

Trolley route

5. Museum of African American History and Culture
6. Magnolia Hall
7. Historic Photos Display
8. Stanton Hall
9. Dunleith
10. Longwood
11. Melrose
12. Monmouth
13. Grand Village of the Natchez Indians

N

Dunleith Mansion

84 Homochitto St.

Lodging and excellent restaurant dining. Reservations recommended—call 800-443-2445. We enjoyed beef tenderloin with lump crab, and molten chocolate for dessert. The mansion, built in 1856, has twenty-six columns around its gallery.

Dunleith mansion.

Natchez National Historic Park

This park operates at three sites in Natchez: **Melrose**, a Greek revival mansion, was completed in 1848. The **William Johnson House** gives valuable insights into the history of the era. Johnson was a slave at birth who was freed at age 11 in 1820. He went on to become a prosperous businessman, landowner, and slaveowner. His diary is fascinating. His home was built in 1841 at 210 State Street. The National Park also protects the remains of **Fort Rosalie**, near 504 South Canal Street.

Grand Village of the Natchez Indians

400 Jefferson Blvd.

Museum, reconstructed mounds and dwellings dated AD 1200 to 1729 are open daily from 9 a.m. to 5 p.m. except for Sunday mornings. 601-447-6502.

Grand Village Mounds

In Natchez, go east off Hwy. 61/Sergeant S. Prentiss Dr. onto Jefferson Davis Blvd., just south of the Natchez Regional Medical Center. Proceed on Jefferson Davis Blvd. half a mile to the entrance gate.

The Grand Village has been designated a National Historic Landmark. Its museum exhibits and interprets artifacts excavated from the site.

Three on-site platform mounds, an adjacent ceremonial plaza and associated habitation areas mark the political and religious capital of the Natchez Indian chiefdom of the late 1600s and early 1700s. Several accounts from French colonists offer rare firsthand glimpses of mound ceremonies.

Elaborate funeral ceremonies, including the sacrifice of relatives and servants of the deceased, were conducted on the mound plaza. Two burials—of the paramount Natchez chief, Great Sun, in 1728 and his brother in 1725—were recorded in historical sources.

The increasing French confiscation of Indian lands led to rapid deterioration of Natchez-French relations

Natchez Under the Hill

A notorious steamboat landing at the Natchez waterfront where gambling, drinking, and brothels abounded. In January 1812, the first steamboat landing in history occurred when the New Orleans, captained by Nicholas Roosevelt,

picked up a small shipment of freight. John Bradbury, an English scientist, visited Natchez in 1812 and described it as amazingly wicked for such a small settlement. John James Audubon visited in 1821. There were originally about five streets leading to the decadent waterfront, but most have since caved into the river. Modern cruising steamboats, a casino, and a historic pub now entice visitors to the Natchez riverfront.

Grand Village Mounds

following the death of the Great Sun. The Natchez attacked nearby Fort Rosalie in 1729. The French retaliated in 1730 by joining with the Choctaw Indians to occupy the Grand Village. The French used the central mound as an emplacement for their artillery. Though the Natchez did not surrender, they permanently abandoned their traditional territory to join other tribes as refugees. Descendants of the Natchez may today be found among the Creek, Cherokee, and Chickasaw Indians.

**Continue south on Hwy. 61 for 34 miles to
Woodville in Wilkinson County.**

Rosemont Plantation

Highway 24 just off Hwy 61. Open Monday through Saturday from 10 a.m. to 4 p.m.

This is the family home of Jefferson Davis. It was built in 1810 by the parents of the future Confederate president and was held by the family until 1895.

NOTES

1 Indian Mounds of Mississippi, A Visitor's Guide. Historic Preservation Division, Mississippi Department of Archives and History. Adapted from the text by Keith Baca.

2 Historic Names and Places, USACE.

3 Historic Names and Places, USACE.

4 Off the Beaten Path, Mississippi by Marlo Carter Kirkpatrick.

5 See Appendix, French Explorers.

6 Milepost designations and descriptions are from the National Park Service.

7 *Mississippi River Panorama.*

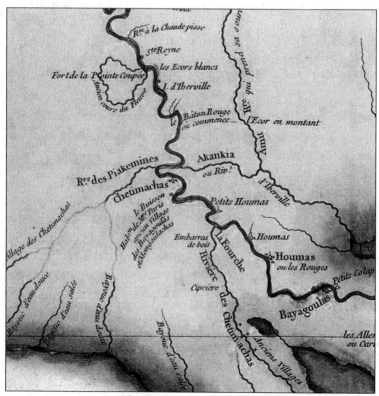

Jean-Baptiste Bourguignon d'Anville. *"Carte de la Louisiane."* 1732.
The Tracy W. McGregor Library of American History.

LOUISIANA

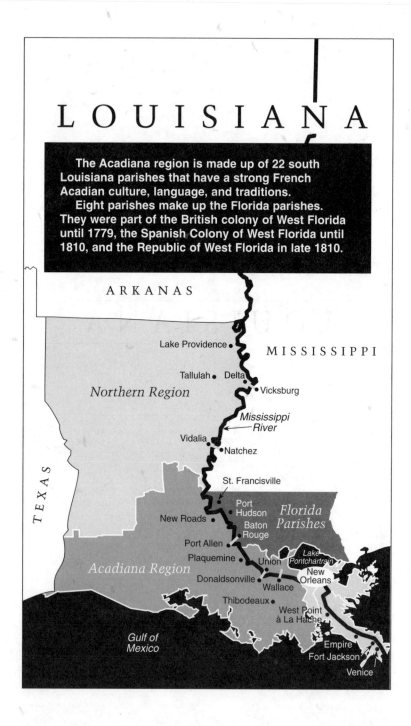

LOUISIANA

The Acadiana region is made up of 22 south Louisiana parishes that have a strong French Acadian culture, language, and traditions.

Eight parishes make up the Florida parishes. They were part of the British colony of West Florida until 1779, the Spanish Colony of West Florida until 1810, and the Republic of West Florida in late 1810.

ARKANAS

MISSISSIPPI

Northern Region

Lake Providence

Tallulah • Delta

•Vicksburg

Mississippi River

Vidalia

•Natchez

T E X A S

St. Francisville

Port Hudson

New Roads •

Florida Parishes

Baton Rouge

Port Allen

Plaquemine •

Union

Lake Pontchartrain

New Orleans

Acadiana Region

Donaldsonville •

Wallace

Thibodeaux •

West Point à La Hache

Gulf of Mexico

Empire

Fort Jackson

Venice

5

A Louisiana Perspective

It was in Louisiana that we truly hit our traveling stride. Good food, a uniquely preserved cultural heritage, well-maintained tourism and recreation sites, well-interpreted historic sites, and easily accessible natural history sites all added to our enjoyment of Louisiana.

The crisp December days were a delight compared to the humidity and heat to be expected during a summer visit. Rains were brief, exciting deluges that pounded on the tin roof of a shack or raged silently outside while we dined in a mansion.

Here in French Louisiana we discovered that a passion for history and family connections has become part of the fabric of life. We met women who still ran their own plantation homes—not managers and staff, but descendants of the same families who had owned their great houses since the eighteenth and nineteenth centuries.

Many locals still feel deep ties to the British, French, Spanish and Caribbean cultures that form the mélange of modern-day Louisiana.

In a version of *Culture 101*, it was explained to us that *Creole* basically means *non-Anglo*. Many Creole consider themselves to be descendants of the great royal families of the French Court of Louis XIV. Their royal ancestors followed hot on the heels of Columbus to develop plantations in the Caribbean—sugar cane, cotton, pineapples—all built on the backs of slave labor.

By the 1740s, after slave revolts in the Caribbean made that life unprofitable, the plantation owners migrated

Good food abounds in Louisiana.

northward to **New France** and eventually established great plantations of indigo and sugar cane on Louisiana's Mississippi River delta. We met families of French ancestry who could tell us which boat and in which year their families arrived in Louisiana during the eighteenth century. These, along with descendents of Africans and Caribbeans, describe themselves as Creole to differentiate themselves from the Germans and Anglo-Americans who settled Louisiana after the Louisiana Purchase in 1803.

The *Acadian (Cajun) French* have an entirely different immigration story. Theirs is one of dislocation and abuse at the hands of the British. During the *Grand Derangement*, following British military victories in Quebec in 1763, French farmers and fishermen from **Acadia** on the northeast coast of Canada were forced to relocate to America's East Coast and eventually to the most inhospitable wetlands of Louisiana—first to St. James Parish, then in a gentle tide throughout the bayous and wetlands of the Mississippi and Atchafalaya river basins.

Swamps and bayous brood just over the next levee throughout Southern Louisiana. Grand baldcypress trees hold court in still, reflective waters with Spanish moss hanging thick in their outspread limbs. On our excursions into the backwaters, we often just sat still, enveloped in silence, except for the slow movement of an alligator submerged to its eyeballs, the squawk of a heron, the scream of a hawk.

Beginning with the Atchafalaya and Red rivers, the Mississippi has dedicated itself to doing what it does most relentlessly in Louisiana—meandering through a broad fan-like *distributary* system to the sea.

Against this epic competitor and galvanized by human losses in the Flood of 1927, the United States Army Corps of Engineers (USACE)has laid its grandest defenses.

Levees, pumping stations, reservoirs, locks, and marinas have all proliferated as the USACE strives to constrain, drain, hold, and reform the river.

But there is more to this river-vs.-Corps epic than what we found at the mouth of the Atchafalaya. There is still the sea. By handicapping the rivers, by rigidly controlling their course, their flow, and their natural rhythms, the Corps has given the sea the upper hand. The incursion of salt water was the number one ecological concern expressed to us by fishermen, farmers, city dwellers, and Cajuns in Louisiana. Louisiana is currently losing nearly twenty-five square miles of land to the sea each year as protective plant life dies and erosion nibbles away at the fragile land mass.

So the battle continues on a new front as the Corps now begins to artificially pump silt-laden river water from the Mississippi and other rivers into oxbows and fields in an effort to reestablish adequate fresh water and soil to hold the land against the sea. One sometimes thinks the Mississippi River had it right all along!!

Inside a Corps of Engineers pumping station.

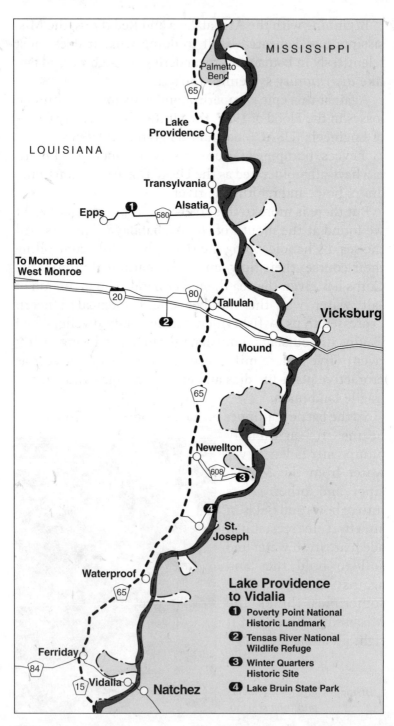

MISSISSIPPI

Palmetto
Bend

65

Lake
Providence

LOUISIANA

Transylvania

Epps ❶ Alsatia
580

To Monroe and
West Monroe

20   80   Tallulah

❷

Mound

Vicksburg

65

Newellton
608   ❸

❹

St.
Joseph

Waterproof
65

**Lake Providence
to Vidalia**
❶ Poverty Point National
    Historic Landmark
❷ Tensas River National
    Wildlife Refuge
❸ Winter Quarters
    Historic Site
❹ Lake Bruin State Park

Ferriday
84

15   Vidalia   Natchez

6

Lake Providence to Waterproof

This portion of our journey through northeastern Louisiana begins at the border between Arkansas and Louisiana on Hwy. 65. There are few major hotels along the Great River Road between Lake Providence and New Roads. We stayed overnight well inland at West Monroe, on I-20. Monroe is a major cultural center for northeast Louisiana, and many national hotel chains are located here. If you have any interest in archeology, do not skip Poverty Point on Hwy 65!

Palmetto Bend ⚓

Mile 326, left bank descending.

The *palmetto* plant, for which this bend is named, is abundant in most of the hardwood forests and swamplands of the Louisiana delta.

Early settlers formed the palmetto into bonnets and fans. While bonnets required that the leaves be dried and pressed and braided into long pieces, making the fans was an easy process. The plant is fan shaped and had only to be dried and trimmed to an appropriate size.

Lake Providence
Population 4,817.

WHAT TO SEE IN LAKE PROVIDENCE

Lake Providence Visitor Center

At the historic Victorian-style Byerly House, 600 Lake Street (Hwy. 65). Open 10 a.m. to 5 p.m.

A well-developed park opposite the Visitor Center offers boardwalk access into a baldcypress swamp—a great stop for picnicking or birding.

Louisiana Cotton Museum

Hwy 65 North. A free exhibit of cotton history in the south. Exhibit of musical instruments of the Delta Blues. 9 a.m. to 5 p.m.

Public Boat Launch

A boat launch and a Bunge North America grain elevator complex south of town offer a good opportunity to see the main channel of the Mississippi. This great river will be mostly invisible unless you make a special effort to find it, and riverside grain elevators are often the best opportunity to do so.

Continue south on Hwy. 65 to Transylvania.

INSIGHT

Grant's Canal at Lake Providence

In early 1863, Federal General Ulysses S. Grant dug a canal here connecting the Mississippi River and Lake Providence as part of his effort to reach Vicksburg via bayous and canals. Grant eventually abandoned his effort to reach Vicksburg by water in favor of a land march.

Transylvania
Population 743.

Transylvania is a small settlement south of Lake Providence. Yes, there is a bat painted on the water tower, and the general store welcomes visitors with a sign that reads "We love fresh blood"! Inquire at the Transylvania Cotton Gin for a tour of the building and cotton ginning process. There are few amenities for travelers.

Follow Hwy. 65 south to Alsatia. Take Hwy. 580 west to Hwy. 577 and then north to Poverty Point Historic Site.

Poverty Point Historic Site (see map on next page)

6859 Hwy. 577, Epps, Louisiana. 318-926-5492. An observation tower allows the visitor a panoramic view of this 400-acre site that protects a group of Indian mounds dating from 1700 to 700 BC. Videos and guided tours at the museum interpret these unique mound structures and artifacts. Small admission fee. Hiking, picknicking. 9 a.m. to 5 p.m.

Construction of the mounds at Poverty Point began 800 years after the Egyptians began construction of the Great Pyramids and well before the construction of the Mayan culture pyramids. The ambitious structures included six rows of concentric ridges nearly 5 feet high that overlooked the Mississippi River flood plain. The outermost ridges were three quarters of a mile long. Two major earthen mounds are still visible, including Poverty Point Mound, a bird-shaped mound measuring 700 by 640 feet at the base and rising nearly 70 feet from the ground.

Located just an hour and a half south of Greenville, Mississippi, the age, size and character of the Poverty Point earthworks makes this historic landmark one of the most significant archeological sites in North America.

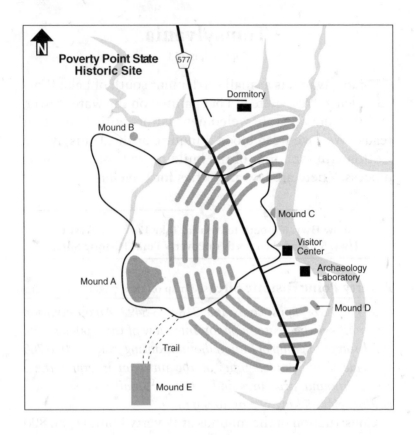

N

Poverty Point State Historic Site

577

Dormitory

Mound B

Mound C

Visitor Center

Archaeology Laboratory

Mound A

Mound D

Trail

Mound E

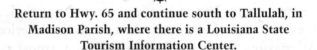

Return to Hwy. 65 and continue south to Tallulah, in
Madison Parish, where there is a Louisiana State
Tourism Information Center.

Tensas National Wildlife Refuge

*Seven miles west of Tallulah on Hwy. 80, then 8 miles south
on the Quebec Road.*

This refuge encompasses 57,000 acres of bottomland forest. Hunting, fishing, hiking, wildlife viewing, canoeing,
interpreted trails, a boardwalk and educational programs
abound. A Visitor Center contains brochures, exhibits,
species lists and regulations.

Return to Hwy. 65 and continue south toward Vidalia, about 70 miles south of Tallulah and across the river from Natchez. Winter Quarters and Lake Bruin State Park are located about halfway between Tallulah and Vidalia.

Winter Quarters State Historic Site

(Mile 400 AHP) Eight miles southeast of Newellton on LA 608 in Tensas Parish, near the Mississippi border. From Hwy. 65, turn onto LA 4 East, then right onto LA 605. After 3 miles, turn left on LA 608. Winter Quarters is approximately 6 miles on the right.

This Civil War historic site features a plantation home on the shores of Lake St. Joseph, a museum, guided tours and special events. 9 a.m. to 5 p.m.

Lake Bruin State Park

From Hwy. 65, take LA 128 east to LA 606 north, then to LA 604. Hwy 604 is located near St. Joseph in the vicinity of Winter Quarters.

Lake Bruin is the Louisiana State Park located closest to the Mississippi River and features beautiful cypress growth along the shores of a 3,500-acre lake. Like many "lakes" along the river, Lake Bruin is actually an oxbow—a sealed-off former bend of the river. Enjoy an interpretive center, swimming, fishing, camping, boat launch, playground, and picnicking.

Notice the shotgun houses along Highway 65 south—so called because you could shoot a gun from the front door to the back door and the bullet would never hit a wall.

111

St. Joseph

St. Joseph (Mile 396 AHP), Highway 128 east, is the county seat of Tensas Parish. Lake St. Joseph is another old bend (oxbow) of the Mississippi. There are a number of antique shops and pre-Civil War buildings in the downtown area.

Waterproof

Waterproof (Mile 381 AHP) is the town that really wasn't! This village relocated from eroding riverbanks four times. Many towns appearing on maps of the Mississippi River delta, like Waterproof, are really just tiny settlements with no visitor amenities. Sometimes the names only commemorate a town that has long since been swept away in the river!

At Clayton, Hwy. 65 merges with Hwy. 15, and Hwy. 65 turns east to Vidalia and then crosses the river into Natchez, Mississippi. To continue south in Louisiana, follow Hwy. 15 south.

Delta Music Museum

Just off Hwy. 65 at 218 Louisiana Avenue (Hwy. 84) in Ferriday (318-757-9999).

Jerry Lee Lewis Family Museum

712 Louisiana Avenue (Hwy. 84). Jerry's sister hosts this museum in her home (318-757-2563).

Vidalia

Vidalia (Mile 357.5 AHP) is a riverfront community about 10 miles east of Ferriday on Hwy. 84. There is a bridge here to Natchez, Mississippi.

Louisiana State Visitor Center

Hwy. 84 near Vidalia, en route to Natchez. 318-336-7008.

If you're staying in Louisiana, continue on Hwy. 15 south until it becomes Louisiana State Hwy. 1 at Lettsworth.

Looking ahead, either New Roads on Louisiana Hwy. 1 or St. Francisville on the opposite bank would be excellent overnight destinations. There is a car ferry crossing between New Roads and St. Francisville (small fee).

Old River Navigation Lock, River mile 304; see page 117.

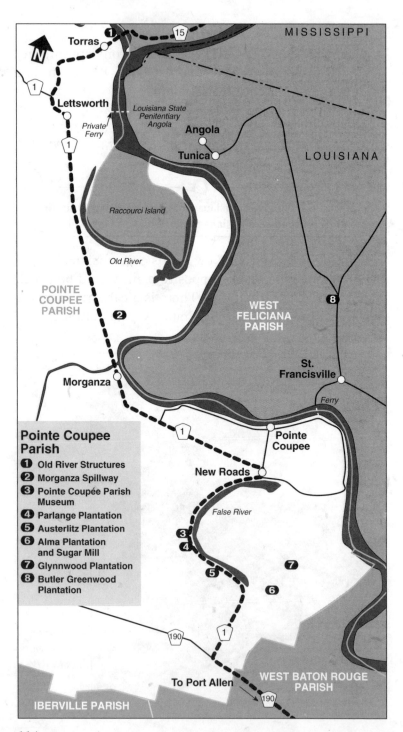

Pointe Coupee Parish

1. Old River Structures
2. Morganza Spillway
3. Pointe Coupée Parish Museum
4. Parlange Plantation
5. Austerlitz Plantation
6. Alma Plantation and Sugar Mill
7. Glynnwood Plantation
8. Butler Greenwood Plantation

7

Pointe Coupée Parish— South Central Louisiana

○

Continue south on Hwy. 15. There are no further visitor attractions until Old River Structures north of Torras.

At Lettsworth, where Highway 15 merges with Historic Highway 1, it is instructive to have a look again at the Louisiana map. At this point, the traveler leaves the northern delta region (originally settled by wealthy East Coast Anglo planters) to become immersed in Louisiana's Creole/Acadian French culture. North and east of Baton Rouge is West Florida, steeped in Spanish, British, and American history progressively.

Beginning here in Pointe Coupée Parish, Louisiana becomes a notable travel delight, rich in history and cultural significance. Culturally, it seems more closely tied to Quebec than the United States, with all the culinary delights and the unself-conscious ethnic pride of the French!

Old River Structures

River mile 314.4. Located on Hwy. 15.

No real visitor amenities, but do stop and have a look at the pumps and the floodway. There is excellent birding

Old River Structures.

in the adjoining wetland and on the road to the Angola ferry, which now operates only for employees of the state prison at Angola.

At the Old River Structures, located at the mouth of the Atchafalaya and Red Rivers, the Army Corps of Engineers closely monitors how much of the Mississippi River is "allowed" to flow down the Atchafalaya basin—30 percent by federal law. For the river buff, this is one of those significant landmarks along the river—on a par with our first visit to Helena, the Vicksburg military park, Natchez, New Orleans, and the end of the Great River Road in Venice.

In recent geologic history, the Red and Atchafalaya Rivers have generally flowed into the Mississippi River, but they also act as *distributaries*, accepting excess water when the Mississippi is in flood. Since the 1880s, however, water has not flowed *into* the Mississippi from either the Red or the Atchafalaya rivers; a portion of the Mississippi has flowed into the Atchafalaya *at all times.*

It eventually became obvious that the Atchafalaya would someday capture the full flow of the Mississippi at the point called "Old River," so in September 1953, Congress authorized the USACE to construct the Low Sill Structure to avert the threatened diversion of the Mississippi.

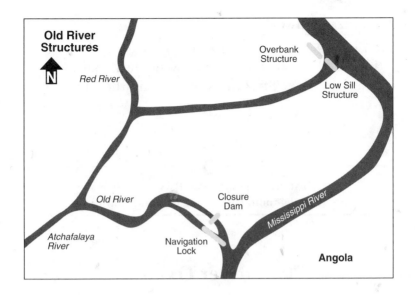

Given its druthers, the Mississippi River today would want nothing more than to return to its ancient haunts in the Atchafalaya Basin. But that would leave Baton Rouge and New Orleans (two of the world's busiest ocean ports) to sugar and cattle plantations, and that, the community figures, is simply unacceptable. So, here at the Old River Structures, the Corps labors to keep the Mississippi grudgingly on its most humanly favored course to the sea.

Old River Navigation Lock

River mile 304.

While there are no locks or dams across the Mississippi River below St. Louis, there are several navigation locks along the river allowing navigation into various tributaries and distributaries. After the Old River Navigation Lock opened to boats entering the Atchafalaya River, the natural channel to the Atchafalaya was closed completely by a huge earthen dam.

The Old River Lock provides passage from the Mississippi into the Old River channel and thence into the Red-Ouachita and Atchafalaya River systems. The lock is 1,185 feet long, 75 feet wide, and has a depth of 11 feet.

Morganza Spillway

River mile 285.7, visible along Hwy. 1.

We found excellent birding between the floodway (seen in the Old River Structures photo) and the Mississippi River.

○

Just before Lettsworth, Hwy. 15 ends.
Turn left onto Hwy. 1 and continue south.

Old River Oxbow

We greatly enjoyed exploring the Old River oxbow north of New Roads, where we found a river camp of buildings on high stilts and a floating tavern, **Big Daddy's Bar and Grill.** Here we found locals—*Cajuns*—who didn't start speaking English until first grade. The parents speak French at home, and at my request, they slipped easily into their native language. Note that the trailer in the picture would not have been high enough to avoid flood damage in 1973!

During that flood, many people we met worked to save the Old River Structures when a whirlpool formed and began to undermine the concrete. They reported that the structure was shaking so badly that a person standing on it swayed back and forth past one standing on solid ground. It took two weeks of round-the-clock work to haul enough rock to fill the hole the whirlpool dug. One fellow at Big Daddy's reminisced that the rocks were so large, sometimes just one rock filled a truck.

Pointe Coupée

Mile 265.5 AHP, right bank.

A French Fort established by Pierre d'Iberville* at Pointe Coupée ("cut point") north of modern-day New Roads had completely disappeared by 1796. Many of Louisiana's earliest sugar cane plantations, some established as early as 1757, were located in this area.

The Marquis de Lafayette, a French statesman and general who volunteered in the continental army during the American Revolution was rewarded by this country with an estate on the Old River oxbow.

New Roads

Population 4,966.

After repeated flooding by the Mississippi River, the people living at the original settlement at Pointe Coupée were forced to build a "new road" to a higher spot a few miles inland. The new settlement was described as being "on the new road" and eventually was simply called New Roads! The jewel of New Roads is the False River Oxbow. Plan to spend the night and enjoy unhurried southern hospitality at its best, pastoral scenery, and great dining with sunwashed lake views.

We stayed at two bed and breakfast inns while in New Roads, **Mon Reve** (225-638-7848) and **Sunrise on the River** (800-644-3642).

We loved our morning sitting on the gazebo-style dock over the False River where we watched the sunrise (of course) at Sunrise on the River. Mon Reve overlooked the False River, and the owner also manages nearly sixty apartments in New Orleans—so if you are looking for a place to stay in New Orleans, call or visit **neworleansb&b.com** for more information.

---

* See index for more on Pierre Le Moyne, Sieur d'Iberville, and his brother Jean Baptists Le Moyne, Sieur de Bienville. Both were born n Montreal, Canada, to Charles Le Moyne.

Sunrise on the River.

It's the people who make all the difference in our travels, and in New Roads we had dinner with three civic leaders at **Satterfield's Restaurant** on the False River. We feasted on fried soft crabs and breaded oysters.

I listened as Glen, Joanna, and another new friend spoke of Pierre d'Iberville's visit in 1699; events in 1729 and 1766; a boat named the *Loire,* and Iberville's shortcut at Pointe Coupée—all as if they had occurred yesterday.

"Wait," I blurted out. "You *do* realize that this is the twenty-first century? You're talking fervently about the early eighteenth century as if it were the war in Iraq!"

Glen paused a moment, taken aback, his pen poised over the napkin spread out over his broad chest so as to form an easel.

"Oh, but you don't realize," Joanna interjected. "Every family represented at this table came on that boat in 1720. So this *is* our story. My goodness, let me tell you about rootedness. Ninety-one percent of those born in Louisiana never leave the state. I have twenty-five first cousins. Only two ever left, and both of us came back!"

Glen and his "easel."

ERNEST J. GAINES

Our visit to New Roads disclosed that **Ernest J. Gaines** grew up in the immediate vicinity. Gaines wrote *The Diary of Miss Jane Pittman,* for which he was a Pulitzer prize runner-up, about life in this area. Plan to pick up a copy to read during your tour of the Lower Mississippi. It is a wonderfully written saga by a man with intimate insight into black heritage in the south. Other books by Gaines include *In My Father's House, A Lesson Before Dying,* and *A Gathering of Old Men.* In 2004, he was nominated for a Nobel prize in literature.

The church from The Diary of Miss Jane Pittman.

Gaines currently resides on a property overlooking the False River in Pointe Coupée. He remembers working in the fields for fifty cents a day when he was nine.

We passed a little white church and an adjoining cemetery that Gaines wrote about in *The Diary of Miss Jane Pittman.*

Fausse (False) River Cutoff

River mile 258.5.

The False River cutoff was mentioned as early as 1699 in the journals of d'Iberville and de Bienville, when one of the accounts mentioned that Indians had informed them of the cutoff and potential time savings should they use it as a portage. The old False River loop was dry except in flood, but was soon lined with homes constructed by some of Louisiana's wealthiest sugar planters.

For more information on New Roads, contact the Greater Pointe Coupée Chamber of Commerce at 800-259-2468 or www.pcchamber.org

Processing Sugar Cane

In Louisiana, we leave the cotton culture behind and sugar cane becomes the major cash crop. Growing and processing sugar cane today is done in a three-year harvest cycle. Cane is planted by burying knotty slips of cane stalk end-to-end in a shallow furrow. The new cane grows from the "eyes" or knots of the old stalk. The growing season is from April to October and cutting is done in the dry season, from October to December. The sturdy cane is harvested in its second and third year.

Today, the process is highly mechanized. Billets—eight-inch pieces of cane—are brought in from the fields by the truckload. Samples are taken from each truck to determine sugar quality, and the proceeds are divided among trucker, farmer, landowner, and sugar mill.

Once the mill starts processing cane, it must operate 24 hours a day until the harvest and processing are completed—if the machinery doesn't run constantly, it will jam up as the sugar syrup hardens. So before processing starts, long truckloads of billets must be ready and waiting. The billets must be washed, and huge piles of mud can be seen around

A mountain of sugar.

sugar mills as a result. Then the main stalks are crushed and syrup is processed from the sap. From the syrup, sugar is produced and refined. According to plantation notes recorded shortly after the Civil War, 12 to 14 tons of ripe cane produced about 1,500 gallons of juice, which resulted in one hogshead of sugar!

Many of the mill workers in Louisiana are Panamanian nationals who dovetail the sugar season in Louisiana with their own in Panama. The skills required to work the mill have largely been lost to local workers.

The end product of the mill we visited was a raw brown sugar that was stored in huge metal barns and moved about with bulldozers like sand or salt! Everywhere was the sweet reek of raw sugar. Abida Rootbeer is made with the local sugar.

One influential resident, Julien Poydras, came to New France in 1768 with only a peddler's backpack. He eventually became very wealthy and participated in the state's first constitutional convention. Poydras was twice elected president of the state senate. At the time of his death, he owned a thousand slaves and six plantations and was considered one of the wealthiest planters in the South.

Today the Fausse (False) River covers more than 4,000 acres and is a favorite hunting, fishing, and boating spot. Several old plantations in the area have been preserved and still operate.

Vertical French log construction, similar to homes still standing in the Ste. Genevieve, Missouri, area, still dot the lower river.

Parlange Plantation

8211 False River Rd., New Roads. 225-638-8410. $10/person Tours by appointment only.

We delighted in meeting Miss Lucy Parlange, mistress of Parlange Plantation. She represented to us a generation of women were truly *genteel*, not just gentle, or kind, or gracious; I remember the baby-soft touch of the hand that held mine tightly while we talked for the first time—and probably the last time—ever!

The Parlange family history reflects the noble beginnings shared by many of the earliest French settlers. Miss Lucy's family history begins with the Countess de Valad, who lived in France from 1650 to 1718 as part of the court of Louis XIV. Her family operated an indigo plantation in Santo Domingo (in the Caribbean) until 1791 after the slave revolts. The Marquis Vincent de Ternant inherited the False River property from his father in the 1750s and built **Parlange.**

The airy raised basement of handmade brick and floors of locally harvested cypress mark the Parlange home as

Parlange plantation.

classic French Creole—likely built by skilled slaves from the Caribbean plantation.

Set in the midst of blooming plants, bamboo shoots, and live oaks on the banks of the False River, this National Historic Landmark plantation is still a working farm surrounded by thousands of acres of sugar cane, corn, soybeans, pecan trees, and pasturelands.

In the front yard, where once there was a formal French garden, two small *pigeoniers*—pigeon houses—still stand. The upper story of each small square structure was used to raise pigeons (squab was a French delicacy!). The lower story of one structure housed the children's tutor, while the French gardener lived in the other. The original Parlange gardener began his career in Le Jardin des Plantes in Paris. Note that the windows of the two dormers were formed of 18 small panes of glass—a good indicator of a home that dates from the mid-eighteenth century.

Miss Lucy pointed out that a portrait by John Singer Sargent of a family member born Virginie Avegno hangs in the Metropolitan Museum today under the title "Madame X" because the Louisiana descendants refused to accept it after it was painted. When her portrait was unveiled in Paris, a provocatively low-cut gown and a strap dangling off her shoulder caused such a scandal that Sargent was forced to move his portrait business from Paris to London.

Sargent himself considered "Madam X" to be a masterpiece. Virginie, born in 1859, was the daughter of a prominent New Orleanian. Her mother was the only surviving child of Claude Vincent de Ternant II, the third owner of Parlange.

"Virginie was a woman considered to be so beautiful that she stopped traffic," Miss Lucy explained. "Ludwig II from Bavaria came to watch her walk up the steps of the Paris Opera. At that same time, she overhead a woman comment that she was beginning to look "worn." She returned home to close herself into a portion of her house that was thereafter kept dimmed and stripped of mirrors.

"I do, however, subscribe to Winston Churchill's observation," Miss Lucy, noted with a wink, "that history is a myth agreed upon."

Pointe Coupée Parish Museum

8348 False River Road (Hwy. 1). Free admission. Open 10 a.m. to 3 p.m.

This museum is one of the few areas where travelers may stop along the False River and enjoy a picnic. There is a picnic table, and the small museum—in an eighteenth-century building—is a work of love. Fishing camps (cabins) are visible across the river.

INSIGHT

Indigo

This deep blue dye used to color cotton and wool was once extracted from the indigo plant. The name *indigo* is a Spanish form of the English word *India*, where the indigo plant, a member of the pea family, is chiefly found.

As early as the twelfth century, southern France was the trade center of *woad*, a purple dye that brought great wealth to those who traded in it. When indigo came onto the market, it offered a far cheaper alternative to woad. Indigo was a major crop on the French plantations in Santo Domingo.

When slave revolts in the Caribbean made production unprofitable, the French planters brought indigo with them to the Mississippi River delta in the 1740s and '50s. The indigo industry disappeared after the Civil War ended as manufacturers began to make synthetic indigo from aniline, a coal-tar product.

Blanche and the Flood of 1927

 When we stayed at Sunrise on the River, Blanche Stowell, a friend of the innkeeper, watched a spectacular sunset with us from the deck. She recalled that during the flood of 1927, her grandfather had built scaffolding inside his family's house so that furniture and belongings could be stored five feet or more above the floors. The scaffolding stayed up for six months, as no one knew when the flood would break through the levee or recede for good. Her father missed the last six weeks of high school because the flood cut off access to the school road, and he was nearly denied entry into Tulane University because he didn't finish that senior year.

Guards patrolled the levees with kerosene lanterns and guns to be sure that farmers from the other river bank did not dynamite the levees. When a levee finally broke in 1927, it was on the bloated Atchafalaya rather than the Mississippi.

Herds of deer became disoriented and drowned as they clambered onto one another's backs, and stranded cattle cried disconsolately. So many animals sought high ground along the roads and levees that it was nearly impossible to drive without hitting them.

Blanche's great-grandfather moved to New Roads from St. James Parish and bought property just above the St. Francisville ferry. All the grandchildren worked in the fields and called the grandparents by the French terms *grand-mère* and *grand-père*. Her grandfather's habit was to be out in the fields before any of the sharecroppers. Blanche's grandmother and great-grandmother were the pharmacists of the day. If sharecroppers became ill, they were called to treat them. If a doctor was necessary, they then called the doctor.

Sharecropping helped planters to overcome cash shortages from after the Civil War through the depression of the 1930s. Sharecroppers got seed and enough credit from landowners to plant a crop and then kept 25 percent as their share. All of the sharecropper's family supplies were purchased at the commissary, where his living expenses pretty much equaled anything he earned.

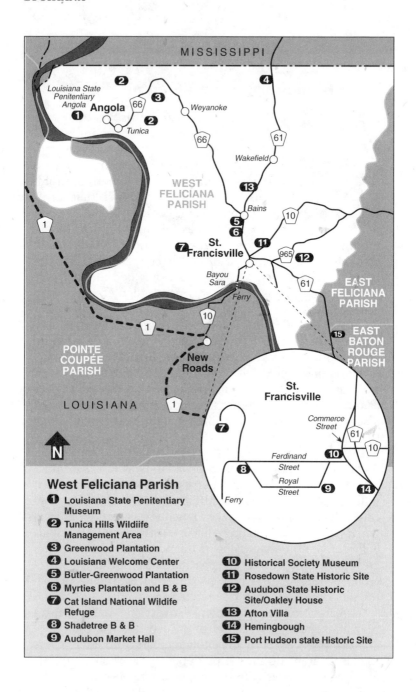

West Feliciana Parish

1. Louisiana State Penitentiary Museum
2. Tunica Hills Wildlife Management Area
3. Greenwood Plantation
4. Louisiana Welcome Center
5. Butler-Greenwood Plantation
6. Myrties Plantation and B & B
7. Cat Island National Wildlife Refuge
8. Shadetree B & B
9. Audubon Market Hall
10. Historical Society Museum
11. Rosedown State Historic Site
12. Audubon State Historic Site/Oakley House
13. Afton Villa
14. Hemingbough
15. Port Hudson state Historic Site

8

West Feliciana Parish

—— ☼ ——

Leave the Great River Road and take Hwy. 10 north in New
Roads to the ferry. Cross the Mississippi to St. Francisville,
in West Feliciana Parish.

A BRIEF HISTORY OF WEST FELICIANA PARISH

The wooded, rolling hills in the vicinity of St. Francisville make this a lovely spot to spend time exploring. The area now known as West Feliciana Parish was
established about 1790 by British and American settlers
on Spanish land grants. To this day, it is the Anglo or
English/American influence that is most noticeable in
West Feliciana rather than the French/Creole culture of
the rest of Southern Louisiana.

When the Louisiana Purchase was negotiated in 1803,
the St. Francisville and Baton Rouge districts were retained
by the Spanish government, which considered them to be
part of the colony of West Florida rather than part of the
Louisiana territory.

The American contingent did not agree and staged a
mini-rebellion, captured the Spanish fort at Baton Rouge
in 1810, and set up the *Republic of West Florida*. The
United States government soon claimed the young

republic, which had established its capitol at a spot across from what is now Grandmother's Buttons on Royal Street in St. Francisville's Historic District.

Follow Hwy. 61 to Bains. Turn left on Hwy 66 and drive to Angola to start your tour of West Feliciana Parish.

Angola, Louisiana
Mile 302.8.
Population 5,456.

Louisiana State Penitentiary Museum

Hwy 66, Angola. The museum is open Monday through Friday from 8 a.m. to 4:30 p.m., on Saturdays from 9 a.m. until 5 p.m., and on Sundays from 1 p.m. until 5 p.m. Gift shop.

The state of Louisiana maintains a penal institution at Angola that has been at the center of a continuing controversy about prison conditions. The prison farm covers about 18,000 acres, much of it in sugar cane. The museum features exhibits detailing 130 years of prison life.

Cat Island National Wildlife Refuge

From Angola, go east on Hwy. 66 and then right on Solitude Rd. Go about 3.5 miles and then turn right at the refuge sign. Follow the signs to the refuge from there (about 1.5 miles). Refuge headquarters can be reached from St. Francisville: From Hy. 61 in St. Francisville, take Commerce St.into town. The office is located at 5720 Commerce St.

Cat Island is actually a point, and a very wet one at that. While the oldest cypress tree in the area is located within this new refuge, frequent flooding often makes the tree inaccessible to hikers. Watch for river otters and enjoy the birding.

Return to Hwy. 66. Turn right and drive to Hwy. 61 at Bains. Turn right and return to St. Francisville. Along this route you will encounter several plantations that are open for public tours: Greenwood, Butler-Greenwood, and Myrtles (see chapter map).

St. Francisville, Louisiana
River mile 265.5.
Population 1,712.

A BRIEF HISTORY OF ST. FRANCISVILLE

In 1730, Capuchin monks from Pointe Coupée on the opposite river bank were using the high loess ridge at St. Francisville as a burial ground. St. Francis was the patron saint of the order, and his name was honored by the little community that grew up around the graveyard. St. Francisville was settled mostly by Anglo-American settlers from the eastern seaboard and became only the second incorporated town in Louisiana in 1807.

Bayou Sara grew up around the riverboat landing just below the city of St. Francisville. While it began as a safe anchorage for flatboats, by 1850 it was the largest steamboat port between New Orleans and Natchez. After the Civil War, river flooding carried away most of the buildings in Bayou Sara. Today, only one building remains of the old town.

Bayou Sara

The Visitor Center and Historical Society Museum

11757 Ferdinand Street. 800-789-4221. ***www.stfrancisville.us.***
The Visitor Center museum is in a restored 1895 hardware store and features excellent interpretive displays. In

St. Francisville's National Historic District Register are 146 homes. Many homes on Royal Street were built in early nineteenth century. A self-guided walking tour begins at the Historical Society Museum, where brochures are available.

This upscale village has many antique shops and boutiques and accommodates frequent visits from the *Delta Queen,* which docks near the ferry landing to New Roads at Bayou Sara.

Grandmother's Buttons

Royal Street.

This shop deserves a visit. Here is a woman with a passion for buttons! While many are originals, the shop also produces replicas for more than 1,200 shops around the country.

ST. FRANCISVILLE PLANTATIONS

St. Francisville was once home to many millionaire plantation owners, and seven plantations in the vicinity remain open to the public (see chapter map for locations). The Audubon Pilgrimage is offered each spring to those interested in tours of the grand mansions.

Many of the plantations are no longer working operations but are still owned by the original families. We especially enjoyed visiting **Oakley House,** where James Audubon worked for a brief few months in 1821 as a tutor and completed many paintings for publication.

The **Shadetree Inn** in St. Francisville turned out to be one of our favorite bed and breakfast inns (225-635-6116). Our shaded porch, perched on the very edge of the Tunica Hills, overlooked the bottoms in the vicinity of Bayou Sara. **The Myrtles B&B** is considered one of the most-haunted mansions in the south. While traveling, we met a man who had stayed at the Myrtles and experienced a gentle nighttime visitor who repeatedly pulled the blanket back over his bare foot! For campers, **Green Acres Campground** is located near the Audubon State Historic Site (Oakley House), 5 miles east on Highway 965 amidst a beautiful heavy forest.

Rosedown State Historic Site

State Hwy. 10 east, St. Francisville. $10 per person. We especially enjoyed a cooking demonstration offered in Rosedown's kitchen on Thursday mornings.

Ninety percent of the furnishings at Rosedown are original to this 1835 home. Because this was a family business headquarters as well as a home, almost every piece of furniture was documented by the original owners, which makes the collection of particular value to historians. Three generations contributed to the development of 28 acres of gardens, which are considered to be comparable with those of the Middleton Gardens in South Carolina.

The marriage of Martha and Daniel Turnbull, the original owners of the plantation, would have combined the resources of two major cotton families. The slave worker economy meant low expenses for production, so there

Cooking demonstration at Rosedown.

USACE Mat Casting Field

St. Francisville has the only mat casting plant still used every year by the USACE. Concrete pieces 3 inches by 2 feet by 3 feet are wired together to form 25-foot lengths called "mats" that are placed along the shores of the Lower Mississippi to prevent erosion. The initial laying of mats on the river banks was completed early in the 1990s. Now the St. Francisville plant is used about three months each year to produce replacement mats.

All the concrete is mixed and the forms are produced on this site. Producing the heavy mats requires highly specialized equipment. For example, whereas once it took 8 men to lift a mat, a machine now does the lifting with just 2 operators. About 7 full-time Corps inspectors work at the plant and 150 to 180 temporary workers are employed when the plant is producing replacement mats. During the 1970s, the plant produced 390,000 mats per year. Over 10 million mats have been produced since the early 1970s.

There is a loading dock beyond a 22-foot levee for loading mats onto the Corps boat that transports them to the replacement location. As each mat is pulled into place on the riverbank by the mat-sinking machine, the mats are automatically wired together. Eighty-five percent of each concrete mattress is under the water, and the portion above the waterline is piled high with stone riprap.

Mats.

really was no claim on the profit other than by the family who owned the plantation. The slave quarters at Rosedown included a dance hall and a church.

Martha Turnbull's daughter, Sarah, willed the home to her four unmarried daughters. There were so few men after the Civil War that many women of the era had no prospects for marriage. Once the cotton industry had been decimated by the boll weevil and increasing cost of labor, the women sold flowers from the gardens, raised chickens for eggs and poultry, and eventually began participating in the annual open houses referred to as "pilgrimages."

While no documentation is available, it is entirely possible that the private restoration of this plantation home between 1956 and 1964 and may have cost $10 million!

Audubon Pilgrimage, St. Francisville, mid-March

The annual Pilgrimage features Oakley, Rural Homestead, Rosedown Gardens, Afton Villa Gardens and four private homes. Visit www.audubonpilgrimage.com or phone 225-635-6330.

The Audubon State Historic Site (Oakley House)

Three miles east of St. Francisville on Hwy. 965.

The Oakley house was built in 1808 by Ruffin Grey. During a brief residency in the home, John James Audubon painted 32 of his "Birds of America" series.

Audubon's four-month stay here in 1821 was in conjunction with tutoring Eliza, the young daughter of the second owner of Oakley. His contract required him to teach half-days, leaving the rest of the day for walking, observing and painting. Subjects included dancing, music, drawing, math, French, and hair-plaiting for $60 per month. Audubon's tight quarters were shared with his 13-year-old assistant.

The home is furnished in the style of the late Federal Period (1790–1830), reflecting its appearance when

Audubon stayed here. One of Eliza's sons married Sarah Turnbull of the nearby Rosedown plantation.

Oakley House.

From St. Francisville, continue south toward Baton Rouge on Hwy. 61 to the Port Hudson State Historic Site.

Port Hudson State Historic Site (River miles 266)

Hwy 61, north of Baton Rouge. Small admission fee.

This site has excellent interpretive displays relating to the Civil War battle that took place here. We especially enjoyed a computer that allowed us to print out and bring home several certificates regarding family-named participants in the Civil War battle of Port Hudson.

Although we hear most often about the 47-day siege of Vicksburg, Port Hudson was the last Confederate stronghold on the Mississippi and also the site of the longest siege in U.S. military history. (Port Hudson's old fortifications

John James Audubon

Audubon arrived in the New World in 1806 from Nantes, France, with Ferdinand Rozier. The two engaged in trading for several years, first in Philadelphia, then down the Ohio River to Missouri. When that partnership dissolved, Audubon returned to Kentucky, where he engaged in a milling venture. When that also failed, the young man was literally forced into the life of artist and ornithologist in order to support his family.

We learned at the Oakley House to appreciate the difference between Audubon's vision and his printer's vision. At left below is Audubon's original painting of red-headed woodpeckers. Notice that he preferred an unembellished background. At the right is a painting of kingfishers that has been embellished by the printer in an effort to make the prints more saleable!

First editions of Audubon's prints are on display at the Oakley great house. During many weekends, visitors can taste food cooked in the original kitchens of the plantation, walk wooded paths, or engage in crafts such as natural dyeing, butter-making or candle-making.

Unadorned Audubon print.

Publisher's embellishments.

Slavery

Interpretive information available along the river indicates that at the time of the Civil War, one-fifth of the American population along the lower river was African. Slavery was present in each of the original 13 states (colonies). While the average plantation had between 10 and 25 slaves, large plantations might have a hundred. Only the single largest slave owner (Julian Poydras on Old River) approached a thousand slaves, and they were distributed over six plantations.

A slave's work schedule usually ran from dawn to dusk six days a week. Slaveholders felt their treatment of slaves was fair and humane and often pointed to the treatment of factory workers in the North as being far less humane. An unattributed quotation describes the life of a young slave boy:

> My life as a slave was spent close to the Kitchen, about 20 feet from the great house. My childhood was spent at play with other children, both colored and white. Occasionally I would see the Master and he would give me something to do sometimes.

> We noticed no difference between white and colored children, nor did they seem to notice any difference. When I began to work, I discovered the difference between myself and my Master's white children. They began to order me about and were told to do so by my Master and Mistress. I found out, too, that they had learned to read, while I was not permitted to have a book in my hand. It was regarded as an offense. I began to have the fear that I would be sold away from those who were dear to me. For us, that was the greatest of all calamities. Our allowance was given weekly: a peck of sifted corn meal, 1.5 dozen herrings, 2.5 pounds of pork. Some of the boys would eat this up in three days and then they would have to steal for the rest of the week. I don't remember one slave but who stole things. They were driven to it by necessity.

I never sat down at a table to eat except at harvest time. In the summer we had one pair of linen trousers given to us, in the winter, one pair of pants, one woolen jacket and two cotton shirts. The slaves are watched by the patrols who ride about trying to catch slaves who are out of their quarters.

Slave cabin.

no longer overlook the Mississippi, as the bends in the river have moved about a mile south of the site.) Six thousand seven hundred Confederate soldiers held off 30,000 to 40,000 Union soldiers under the command of General Nathaniel P. Banks from May 23 to July 9, 1863. The soldiers did not surrender until after they learned that Vicksburg, 160 miles away, had surrendered on July 4.

With the defeat of Port Hudson, the Mississippi River was finally open to the Union fleet from end to end. This was also the first battle in which free black soldiers fought alongside Union soldiers. Wisconsin, Michigan, and New York provided the bulk of the Union soldiers.

The National Cemetery at Port Hudson contains the bodies of 3,804 Union soldiers. Nine hundred acres of battlefield are protected by the site, and six miles of hiking trails meander among the battlefield formations.

This water cistern at Woodland plantation is a ruin from the nine-teenth century.

Come back to this picture after finishing your journey. You will know why this early nineteenth century home has two front doors (one for men and another for women). You'll know these entries were called brisées *by its original* Creole *owners. You'll know that it probably had a large* gallery *or porch and 18 small panes of glass produced on-site in each of the four windows of the dormers. There's also a good chance that this was the overseer's home!*

Port Allen Lock and Canal

Along Hwy. 61 into Baton Rouge and the Intracoastal Waterway, Mile 228.4, Right Bank Descending.

This USACE Canal cuts the distance from the Mississippi River to the western branch of the Gulf Intracoastal Waterway by 160 miles. The locks here replaced the obsolete lock at Plaquemine, Louisiana.

The Intracoastal Waterway is 1,109 miles long and stretches from the Mexican border around the Gulf of Mexico to Apalachee Bay in Florida. In 1942, 13 German U-boats were discovered in the Gulf of Mexico, which made the inland Intracoastal Waterway of great importance.

9

Baton Rouge

A BRIEF HISTORY OF BATON ROUGE

The capital city of Louisiana was first noted as Baton Rouge nearly three centuries ago when French explorer Pierre Le Moyne d'Iberville visited the area and found a red-painted stick (most likely a tall tree snag stripped of its branches) that was said to mark the boundary between two Indian nations. A small military post was established there and a large plantation was developed on a Spanish land grant. After Baton Rouge was ceded to the British by France at the end of the Seven Years War, it housed a British garrison. During the Revolutionary War, it was overwhelmed again and held by the Spanish until 1810, when the American element joined the rebellion and made Baton Rouge part of the independent Republic of West Florida.

Three months later it was annexed by the American government, and Baton Rouge became an American city. The old dirt fort came under the command of Army Colonel Zachary Taylor. Taylor was a general in both the Mexican War and the Black Hawk War in Wisconsin. He became president of the United States in 1849.

Today the Port of Baton Rouge is located at the head of the deepwater channel that leads to the Gulf of Mexico via New Orleans. This stretch of river is highly

Historic waterfront.

industrialized, with large chemical plants, grain elevators and petroleum refineries in the Baton Rouge area. Baton Rouge is the nation's seventh largest port, and the river between Baton Rouge and the Gulf of Mexico is crowded with ocean-going vessels and towboats. According to the USACE, there is no marina for pleasure boaters, and boaters should be extremely careful in the area.

WHAT TO SEE IN BATON ROUGE
Baton Rouge Area Convention and Vistors Bureau,
800-La-Rouge or 225-383-1835.

Hotels and two casino riverboats line the riverfront in Baton Rouge. Also of interest downtown are

Louisiana State Capitol

State Capitol Drive.
   Completed in 1932, the Art Deco style building is the tallest capitol in the nation.

Old State Capitol Museum

100 North Blvd. at River Road
This museum houses the Center for Political and Governmental History.

Louisiana Arts and Science Museum

100 S. River Rd.
This museum includes art exhibits, an Egyptian tomb and mummies, a simulated space station, and more.

U.S.S. Kidd and Nautical Museum

305 S. River Road.
The *U.S.S. Kidd* is a restored World War II destroyer. The Nautical Museum features artifacts, a submarine exhibit, and gift shop.

Argosy Casino and Casino Rouge

On the riverfront near the Sheraton Hotel.

The LSU Rural Life Museum and Windrush Gardens

4600 Essen Lane (at I-10). Baton Rouge. Closes at 5 p.m.
This huge museum complex is housed in 23 buildings and depicts the various cultures of pre-industrial nineteenth-century Louisiana. It is not to be missed! In addition to plantation buildings, shotgun houses, overseer offices, and slave quarters, we saw a dogtrot log cabin (two cabins adjoined by a "dogtrot" or open breezeway), an Acadian home, and the normal accoutrements of rural life in the eighteenth and early nineteenth centuries.

Interpretive displays remind us that the agricultural community included yeomen—working farmers who operated small holdings without the benefit of slaves. These were often British loyalists from America's east coast.

A Cajun home with the over-hang porch. In the backyard are an on-ground cistern and a sugar press very similar to what we saw Indian natives using along the Amazon River!

A Towboat Pilot's Note to Boaters

I've been in the business of piloting riverboats for nearly thirty years now and have worked on all the Western rivers and the Lower Mississippi in particular during most of that time. I returned early this year from nearly six years, working on the Orinoco, the Parana, and the Paraguay rivers in South America.

I would like to remind you of the dangers of pleasure boating on the Lower Mississippi between St. Louis and Head of Passes. Please, *please,* do not ever underestimate the river. I have seen it kill far too many people—friends, strangers, professional rivermen, amateur boatmen, women, and children. I have seen more foolishness than you could ever comprehend, more often than not perpetuated by people who hadn't a clue regarding their own behavior.

I have seen all sorts of noncommercial vessels, from million-dollar cruisers to rafts to canoes to two twelve-year-old boys navigating Luling Bridge on a log.

I have to tell you that what these people usually inspire in me is fear. I would rather encounter a snake in my bathtub than an imbecile riding my wheelwash on a Jet Ski. I wouldn't mind killing the snake; regarding the imbecile, I'd feel—well—conflicted. That's sick humor, of course. The truth is, it would probably wreck my life as surely as killing a child with my car would do.

Our standard tow, southbound, is usually 30 barges, 50,000 tons or so, distributed over a 5-acre area. By law, southbound traffic has the right-of-way. But whether you are northbound or southbound in your pleasure craft, I cannot always maneuver in order to avoid you, not with a heavy tow on my head and the current at my back, and certainly not in a restricted channel—and while the river may seem as wide as the ocean from the deck of a houseboat, from my point of view every channel between St. Louis and New Orleans is a restricted channel to some extent. And there are many places where I literally cannot stop my tow, particularly during high water, where to attempt it would place millions of dollars of cargo and equipment, as well as the lives of my crew, in danger. Given the most fortunate of circumstances, with a moderate current, I need about half a mile to stop completely—dead in the water.

Commercial traffic is not the only danger to travelers. I have seen drift—logs and such—knock holes in the steel hulls of barges; imagine what a big blue cypress log would do to a fiberglass hull! And assistance during an emergency is hard to come by on the Lower River. Given liabilities and legalities, I'm not apt to lower my launch and put my own crew in jeopardy except to answer an emergency, and, such are the dangers, I would be very reluctant to ask my boys to risk their lives at night in a small boat to save *anyone*. Even for us, help is often hard to reach.

It is not my intention here to frighten people, but merely to persuade them to plan their trips intelligently, with these warnings in mind. My advice is to have some means of communications, such as a VHF marine radio. Channel 16 is the call and distress frequency, and we are all required to monitor that channel, but if you want to talk to us you would be better advised to use channel 13, the navigation channel on which most of our business is conducted. I won't say that all of my fellow pilots and captains are as courteous as your local bus driver—we don't think about public relations as much as we ought to, sometimes—but we are, uniformly, a pretty professional bunch, and all of us know far more about the river than the casual traveler is ever apt to know.

We are a resource you can employ only if you have the means of communicating with us. And no one can help you if you do not know where you are— "on the river" isn't good enough. Buy a chart; the new lower Mississippi charts are the biggest darned charts I've ever seen, but they are the easiest to read and include all the navigation lights and requisite place names.

Traveling the river is actually a wonderful and rich experience for anyone. There is richness to those place names and to the language we pilots use and have used for nearly two hundred years now. The traveler may even discover that he has been not merely tourist, but a witness, to the life of the river.

*A towboat with nagivation sign. The navigation sign shown in the photo is referred to as a "daymark" on the river. Daymarks may be in red or green. If they are in the shape of a square or a triangle, they are called "passing daymarks," indicating that the channel is passing closer to that shore than the other shore. If the daymark is in the shape of a diamond, it is referred to as a "crossing daymark." These indicate that the channel is crossing from one side of the river to the other. For more information on navigating the Mississippi River, visit **www.greatriver.com/ order.htm** and request a copy of* A River Companion *by Karen "Toots" Maloy.*

Mississippi River view. This is one big river!

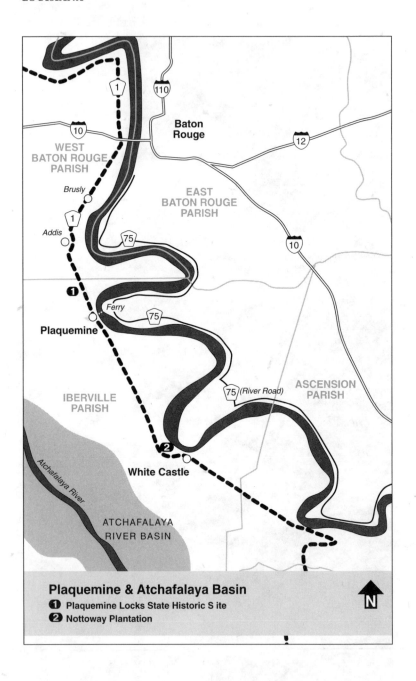

Plaquemine & Atchafalaya Basin
❶ Plaquemine Locks State Historic S ite
❷ Nottoway Plantation

10

Plaquemine &
the Atchafalaya Basin

○

From Baton Rouge, take Interstate 10 west toward the
Mississippi River. On the Mississippi River bridge, get in
the middle lane. Take the first exit, onto Hwy. 1,
and drive south to Plaquemine. A car ferry crosses the
Mississippi at Plaquemine from 5 a.m. to 9 p.m.

Plaquemine
Mile 208.6 right bank descending

Plaquemine sprang up in about 1800 along the Bayou
Plaquemine. The name Plaquemine is derived from
piakemens, said to be an Indian word referring to a
persimmon-like tree. Persimmons are quite common to
the area. The orange fruit of this small tree becomes quite
sweet when ripe.

By 1909, Plaquemine was a flourishing town. Paddle-
wheeled steamboats moved Spanish moss, cotton, grains,
sugar cane, lumber, and seafood products though the
Plaquemine Lock. Locals swam in the locks and did
shrimping just outside the lock.

Plaquemine's historic district stretches along Railroad Avenue. The City Café has been there since 1919. The historic locks on the Bayou Plaquemine are well worth a visit for the interpretive displays, small boat museum, and a well developed Bayou Waterfront Park.

Plaquemine Locks State Historic Site

57730 Main St., Plaquemine.

The navigation lock built by Colonel George W. Goethals and completed in 1909 is no longer in use, but it is open to the public and operated by the state of Louisiana as one of four historic sites along the Great River Road. The lock connecting the Mississippi River and Bayou Plaquemine provided a lift of 51 feet, the highest freshwater lift in the world in 1909. It was last used in 1961 and was replaced by the Port Allen locks. Colonel Goethals would eventually become chief engineer for the building of the Panama Canal.

Plaquemine Lock.

The lock site includes the original lockhouse and a visitor center. A visit to the Gary James Hebert Memorial Lockhouse, a boat museum on park grounds across from the lock, is highly recommended.

The *pirogue* in the photo is representative of boats commonly used by individuals in the bayous. They were often carved out of a single baldcypress log. We have seen

A pirogue in the boat museum.

natives on the Amazon River using identically made boats!

Plaquemine Locks is also a convenient location to climb the levee for a view of the Main Mississippi River channel. A Dow chemical plant along the riverbank nearby produces such plastic products as Ziploc® bags. The riverbank from Baton Rouge to New Orleans is lined with chemical plants and has become known as the "Chemical Corridor."

LOUISIANA'S RIVER ROAD

The levee road (Highway 75) between Baton Rouge and New Orleans has long been called the River Road, not to be confused with the federally designated Great River Road. The levee blocks views of the river most of the time, but many River Road plantations are open to the public. At one time, all of the plantation homes would have had unimpeded river views.

Nottoway Plantation

Off of Hwy. 1 at 30970 Hwy. 405 south of Plaquemine and just north of White Castle. Phone 866-4-avisit.

Nottoway is noted for its fine restaurant and lodging. The ostentatious white columned plantation home reflects the Anglo-American influence compared to the Creole cottages of the French. The overseer's cabin and the household quarters are now bed and breakfast accommodations. There are no other hotels in the immediate area of Plaquemine, although there are hotels in Port Allen and Donaldsonville.

We had a delicious turkey and sausage gumbo at Randolph Hall, Nottoway's restaurant. The crawfish étouffée, seafood platter salad, and bread pudding were all also excellent. Johnnie Jambalaya is typical of the "showboat" chefs that we found featured increasingly at fine restaurants as we neared New Orleans. His product line included franchised bottles of dressing, flavorings, and a CD with music and recipes. Louisiana cuisine is his specialty.

The original owner of Nottoway made his fortune in sugar cane and completed the home in 1859. The Greek Revival, Italianate-style mansion had 64 rooms within its 53,000 square feet and required 15 to 20 slaves to oper-

Nottoway Plantation house.

A delicious meal at Nottoway's Randolph Hall.

ate. The plantation sat on 7,000 acres of land and was worked by perhaps 176 slaves. It is considered to be the largest plantation home in the South. Today, as with other plantations in the area, the levee separates Nottoway from its former river vista.

Inside the mansion, the elaborate friezework (decorative sculpted borders) is the most notable aspect of Nottoway's design.

The home survived the Civil War because the captain of the first gunboat that passed realized he had once been a guest there. The family was allowed to stay in the home, and he had soldiers pitch their tents along the river so that other passing gunboat captains would believe the home was already occupied.

Continue south on Hwy. 1. As you do so, you'll notice that bayous and wetlands become prominent. To the west of Hwy. 1 is the Atchafalaya Basin, 20 miles wide east to west and 150 miles north to south.

INSIGHT

Plantations Were Mostly Self-Sufficient

A plantation home might have French chandeliers, but its window glass was made on-site. Mattresses in the home would have been stuffed with Spanish moss. The plantation may have been lighted with gas lamps, the gas produced by dripping water on calcium carbide to produce acetylene gas.

Atchafalaya Basin

The Atchafalaya Basin is a vast area of swamp, woodland, bayou, and marsh covering more than 1.4 million acres. It is the largest freshwater swamp and contains the largest bottomland hardwood forest in the nation.

More than 100 species of fish and crustaceans swim in the still waters of the Atchafalaya River Basin. It is considered to be five times more productive than the Florida Everglades. Our guide, Dean Wilson, assured us that yes, alligator gar weighing as much as 300 pounds commonly cruise these bayous along with 150-pound alligator snapping turtles.

Nutrias, beavers, deer, and bobcats live on higher ground along the bayous while bald eagles, ospreys, egrets, and other large water birds will be seen perched in the magnificent baldcypress or stalking their next meal in the still waters. Many locals still hunt and fish off the land. Wilson told us that he sometimes catches crested cormorants (diving birds) in his nets when he fishes. Disentangling them is a challenge, as they are very quick and lethal with their bills and invariably go for the eyes of their captors.

Baldcypress in the Atchafalaya Basin

Wilson showed us the extremely small flower of the Spanish moss that was blooming during our early December visit. The physiology of the flower makes it a relative of the pineapple plant!!

Wilson, who grew up in Spain and still carries a distinctive accent, arrived in Louisiana 18 years ago after seeing a *National Geographic* story on the Atchafalaya River basin. His original plan was to use his Atchafalaya experience to pre-

Dean Wilson shows us a Spanish moss flower.

pare him for eventually living on the Amazon River in South America, but the Atchafalaya became his home and the Amazon plan never materialized.

His love for the bayou, the swamp and marsh, and the baldcypress in particular is obvious. While natural streams once flowed throughout the basin, many canals were dredged out to provide access to boats and pipelines operated by the oil and gas companies. He pointed out the high banks of the artificial canals and the low, flood-prone banks of the natural waterways.

He noted sadly that it is highly unlikely that the regal baldcypress will survive the hand of man in the great basin. Harvesting of baldcypress was already intense during the days of the French, but peaked at the turn of the twentieth century, when much of the basin was clear-cut of virgin cypress timber. The wood of baldcypress is exceptionally

bayou: The word derives from the Choctaw Indian word for a slow, meandering waterway. Look for live oaks on the high ground along bayous. In lowland areas baldcypress and tupelo swamps are most common; *flotant* marsh occurs where land is slowly sinking and water begins to cover it permanently.

resistant to rot and is sought after for boats, jetties, houses, and lumber that might come in contact with water.

The largest lumber company on the east side of the basin in the early twentieth century was located at Plaquemine, so the bayous near there would have been among the first to be harvested. Any large trees standing today would have been rejected then as too hollow, unhealthy, or small for commercial harvesting.

Huge stumps of harvested trees still clutter the bayous. While the water- and rot-resistant qualities of baldcypress lumber make it extremely popular for construction, it also means that stumps take an inordinately long time to decompose.

Harvesting of the cypress continues today, and as soon as the trees grow to a diameter of 2 feet at about 4 feet above the water, they may be harvested. As Wilson pointed out, the baldcypress is naturally wide at the bottom but rapidly becomes very slim—thus virtually every tree is a candidate for harvesting. A fully mature baldcypress would probably be 15 feet in diameter 4 feet above the water.

In addition, willow trees originally planted along the levees for erosion control have spread throughout the basin

and are harvested for pulpwood. Because willows grow so aggressively, it is unlikely that young baldcypress will be able to compete for space and light— they simply grow too slowly.

In addition to guiding visitors to

Huge baldcypress stumps dot the basin.

Harvesting baldcypress in the early nineteenth century.

the Atchafalaya basin, Wilson is a commercial fisherman, trapper and hunter. During one unusually lucrative crawfish season he earned $700 a day! When the fish run, a day's catch might weigh 1500 pounds. However, market prices for catfish and crawfish have dropped precipitously due to imports from China and Vietnam. Fifty years ago, catfish brought the commercial fisherman as much as 70 cents per pound. Today rough fish bring only 10 to 45 cents per pound.

Wilson pointed out that the bayou water appeared to be full of moving ridges that made the smooth surface of the still water undulate. This disturbance was caused by the movement of huge schools of fish. He explained that

A cypress today.

they were collecting in the bayous because they sensed that there would soon be flooding, which would release them to feed thoughout the swamps and marshy areas. "I know there's high water coming because I can look at a computer forecast. How they know is a puzzle to me," he said.

He took us into an area where he knew there were three alligators. Sure enough, we saw them—or at least their knobby eyes and snouts. When we came too close, even the eyes and snouts disappeared—ever so slowly, ever so silently.

Wilson firmly believes that he has seen a pair of ivory-billed woodpeckers—long thought by others to be extinct—on three occasions in the past ten years. He recognizes the ivory-billed by its distinctive white bill, the pattern of white on its wings, and its exceptionally large size. The female ivory-billed has a black crest, while the female pileated has a red crest. He has seen both male and female birds, and all his sightings have been in the spring, so he feels that they might just be migrating through. While he has been listening for their call for eight years, he has never heard it.

Wilson related that when one of his friends on the Pearl River showed a picture of an ivory-billed to his grandmother, she identified it easily: "Of course—that's a wood turkey. They are very good eating."

Wilson operates Last Wilderness Tours, and we greatly enjoyed our visit. But there are dozens of other tours recommended throughout southern Louisiana. Reserve your tour in advance by calling one of the tourism contacts in the Appendix.

INSIGHT

Harvesting Baldcypress

By 1900, the area around New Orleans had been virtually stripped of virgin baldcypress trees. They grew straight and tall, up to 150 feet high and over 15 feet in diameter.

In order to harvest the baldcypress it was necessary to strip away the outer bark in a girdle around the trunk at least a year before harvesting. By harvest time, the tree would have dried substantially and thus would be easier to cut and float out of the bayou. We visited a woman whose brothers all worked for a nearby lumber company. She said that her father had harvested baldcypress in the swamps, sometimes wading through chest-high water.

*"Harvesting of the cypress continues today,
and as soon as the trees grow to a diameter of
2 feet at about 4 feet above the water,
they may be harvested. . . . the baldcypress is
naturally wide at the bottom but rapidly becomes
very slim—thus virtually every tree
is a candidate for harvesting."*

Alligator Gar

The awesome *alligator gar* first came to my attention when I visited Reelfoot Lake in Tennessee. These prehistoric monsters reach 300 pounds and over 6 feet in length rather frequently! Once found as far north as the Ohio River, their numbers are dwindling. I learned that they are among the most vicious creatures in the river. I've spoken to alligator gar fishermen who use a 2x4 board as a "bobber" and wire for fishing line!

This photo of a preserved gar head illustrates exactly why it is called an alligator gar! It is an aggressive fish with alligator-like teeth. Many people who think they have been attacked by an alligator have really had an encounter with an alligator gar!

Compare the monsters above with the needlenose gar commonly found in the Upper Mississippi.

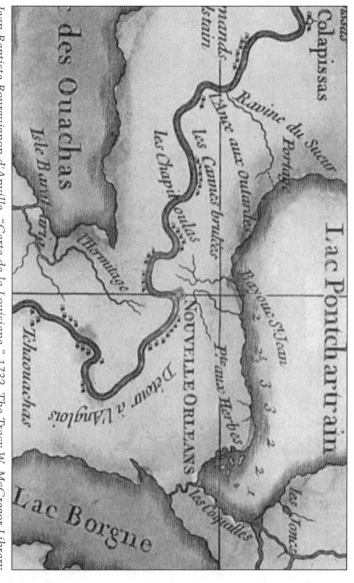

Jean-Baptiste Bourguignon d'Anville. "Carte de la Louisiane." 1732. The Tracy W. McGregor Library of American History. Compare this 1732 map to the map on page 164.

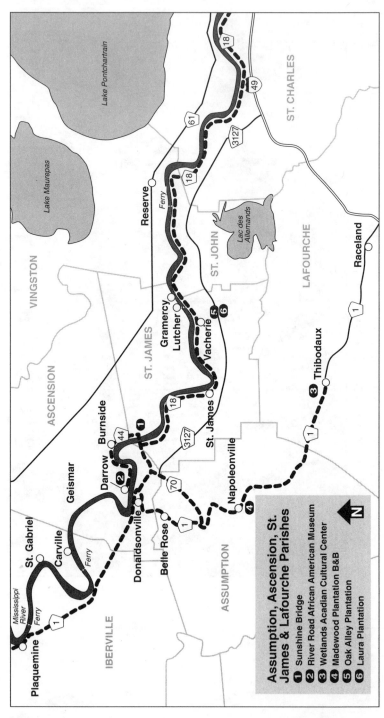

Lake Pontchartrain

Lake Maurepas

ST. CHARLES

18

49

61

3127

18

Reserve
Ferry

Lac des
Allemands

ST. JOHN

LAFOURCHE

Raceland

1

LIVINGSTON

Gramercy
Lutcher
Vacherie

5

6

ST. JAMES

Thibodaux

3

ASCENSION

Burnside

Darrow

44

18

1

3127

St. James

Napoleonville

4

1

Geismar

70

St. Gabriel

Carville

Ferry

Donaldsonville

Belle Rose

1

ASSUMPTION

IBERVILLE

Mississippi
River
Ferry

1

Plaquemine

N

**Assumption, Ascension, St.
James & Lafourche Parishes**

1 Sunshine Bridge
2 River Road African American Museum
3 Wetlands Acadian Cultural Center
4 Madewood Plantation B&B
5 Oak Alley Plantation
6 Laura Plantation

11

Assumption, Ascension, St. James & Lafourche Parishes

LOUISIANA'S "GERMAN COAST"

Between 1718 and 1722 Scottish financier John Law recruited a large number of Germans to settle the Louisiana colony on behalf of his "Company of the West." Many were German indentured servants who traveled with Law to the mouth of the Arkansas River to work his plantation-empire, which he represented as being far more successfully developed than it actually was!

When Law's "Mississippi Bubble" burst, most immigrants headed back downriver hoping to find passage to Europe. Jean Baptiste de Bienville, the French governor of the colony, persuaded many to settle on the river above present day Geismar. This area became widely known for its prosperous little towns. Swiss, Spanish, and American planters soon joined the Germans.

We met a family from Connecticut whose reunion in Louisiana centered on family property located near the Woodland Plantation at near West Pointe à la Hache, south of New Orleans, but they had ties to the German Coast. An ancestor, a German immigrant, found a job delivering mail from a mail boat along the German Coast. Somewhere along the route he met Thomas Edison, who encouraged him to become an inventor. He did, and in time he became wealthy enough to buy a plantation near the Woodland plantation. The success of early settlers was often merely a matter of chance.

From Plaquemine, continue on Hwy. 1 to Donaldsonville.

Donaldsonville
River mile 175.2
Donaldsonville Tourism, 225-473-4814

Donaldsonville, located where Bayou La Fourche enters the Mississippi River, was the site of a trading post by 1750 and an Ascension Catholic Church built in 1772 by the French Acadian settlers. In 1806, William Donaldson acquired a large tract and laid out a town on the riverbank that came to be called "La Ville de Donaldson." For a full three-month term in 1830, Donaldsonville served as the capital of Louisiana. Donaldsonville elected Pierre Landry its first African American mayor in 1868. Fats Domino, Joe King Oliver, and other performers all played in Donaldsonville. Today it is surrounded by sugar cane and soybean operations.

**East of Donaldsonville, cross the Mississippi
on the "Sunshine Bridge" (Hwy. 70). Turn left on Hwy. 44
and follow it to Darrow.**

Sunshine Bridge—the Bridge to Nowhere!

The Sunshine Bridge, which crosses the Mississippi on Highway 70 east of Donaldsonville, was once called the "Bridge to Nowhere" because the east side of the river wasn't developed. Now you'll see increasing economic development around its eastern ramps.

Crossing any Mississippi River bridge south of Baton Rouge is an event! Each must be high enough to allow ocean ships to pass underneath, and the exit ramps spread far out over neighboring fields.

Darrow

River Road African American Museum

3138 Hwy 44, Darrow, LA 70725. Located opposite Donaldsonville on the east bank of the river, just over the Sunshine Bridge.

Kathe Hambrick is the founder, director, and curator of the River Road African American Museum. She hopes to expand the museum into Donaldsonville and hopes to develop several other properties that she holds in trust.

"I've been doing this a long time," she tells us. "Suddenly black history is cool. Everyone sees a nickel to be made. My mission here is to interpret black history, not exploit it. I'm really not interested in seeing Disney do Black history."

Return to the west side of the river via the Sunshine Bridge. Take Hwy. 70 through Donaldsonville and return to to Hwy. 1 for an interesting side trip. Turn left (south) on Hwy. 1 and continue to Thibodaux.

Thibodaux

The town of Thibodaux is located at the junction of Highway 20 and Highway 1. This interesting side trip through the Acadian interior south and west of Vacherie and the Great River Road is highly recommended.

Wetlands Acadian Cultural Center

314 Mary St., Thibodaux. The building is located directly on the Bayou La Fourche when you cross the bridge at Thibodaux. It is easy to miss. The site includes an excellent museum, a boardwalk along the historic Bayou LaFourche, a gift shop. and more.

This exceptional Acadian culture interpretive center is well worth an excursion off the Great River Road. Displays are outstanding, and the center houses an excellent regional bookstore. The boardwalk was a comfortable path to walk along to see the bayou. Bayou La Fourche enters the Mississippi River at Donaldsonville. See the Appendix for a timeline of the Acadians in Louisiana.

Continue on Hwy. 1 to Raceland to visit its sugar mill.

Raceland Sugar Mill

Raceland, Hwy. 1/308. Public tours offered.

Sugar cane, rice, and cotton offer another interesting parallel between the northern and southern extremities of the Mississippi River—compare, for example, the wild rice savannas of northern Minnesota to the cultivated rice fields of Louisiana. Maple syrup on the Upper Mississippi is replaced by the sugar cane on the Lower; while the hemp and flax of Iowa and Wisconsin are paralleled by the cotton of Mississippi and Arkansas.

INSIGHT

Raising Cane

Today, this general area is one of the most productive sugar cane areas in Louisiana. Reserve, north of the Mississippi on Interstate 10 (at the west end of Lake Pontchartrain), ws long home to **Godchaux Refinery,** one of nation's largest sugar companies.

As early as 1725 French settlers tried and failed to produce sugar. They turned to indigo and cotton as export crops, but by the end of the century indigo had been destroyed by insects and cotton was too expensive to produce.

In 1795, Etienne de Bore made a desperate decision to try sugar once more. His success, and an influx of refugees from the Santo Domingo slave revolt, gave impetus to the local industry. Skilled Caribbean slaves were familiar with sugar culture. By 1827 there were 308 sugar estates in Louisiana, employing about 21,000 slaves. By 1849, there were 1,536 sugar plantations employing more than 100,000 slaves.

When we visited the area, Nelson Melancon, whose father and grandfather were also cane farmers, was harvesting his 300 leased acres of cane with a huge piece of machinery. Just two men were doing the work that once employed dozens in desperately difficult labor. Today the cane goes from field to refinery untouched by human hands.

Three hundred acres, Nelson suggested, is a small farm, yet it provides a "good living." A farmer might get $6 a ton for the results of his harvest, which are measures in tons of billets—6- to 8-inch bits of green cane.

A woman across the street from the cane field waved us over. She lives on a small strip of land once owned by her mother with her nine brothers. Her brothers all worked for the lumber company where her dad had worked clear-cutting cypress in the 1920s. She commented that mechanizing the sugar cane harvest cost a lot of people their jobs.

✪

Retrace your tracks back to Napoleonville on Hwy. 1/308.

Napoleonville

Madewood Plantation B&B

4250 Hwy. 308 (Hwy. 1), Napoleonville.

We spent the night here before returning to the river. Madewood Plantation is a classic example of the Anglo style of architecture, with a columned entry and white stone. It's estimated that more than 600,000 handmade bricks were used to build the home. Our evening dinner here was delicious.

✪

Continue north on Hwy. 1/308 to Hwy. 70. Turn right and proceed almost to the Sunshine Bridge, where you'll turn right on Hwy. 18, also known as the River Road or Levee Road. The towns along this stretch are small and don't offer many tourist attractions, but there are many plantations in the area (see plantation map on pages 172–73).

Madewood Plantation B & B.

St. James Parish

Many months have slipped away since we returned from our Louisiana visit, but I am still telling the stories of our Cajun/Creole adventure—stories about the "Grand Derangement" of Nova Scotia's Acadians in 1755 and their subsequent resettlement in the Louisiana bayous. About Jean Lafitte, the gentleman privateer whose jewels and doubloons are remembered today in the yellow, green, and purple plastic beads that drape Canal Street trees after the Mardi Gras parades. I share the foot-stompin' Cajun fiddle music of David Greeley with my fiddlin' neighbor, Dan; the "hot Jazz" of Banu Gibson with my daughter.

A BRIEF HISTORY OF ST. JAMES PARISH

The area around the community of St. James may be the site of the earliest Acadian settlement in Louisiana. The Acadians were exiled from Nova Scotia by Britain in 1755. They began arriving in Louisiana in 1763 or '64 after extreme hardship. By 1768 there were 500 French-speaking Acadians in Louisiana, followed by another 2,500 in a movement described as *Le Grand Derangement.* Today about half a million peo- 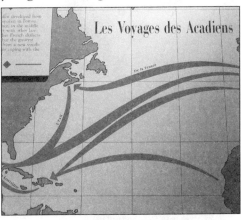 ple in Louisiana are descended from the Acadian (Cajun) settlers.

A plaque at St. James church on Highway 18 reads:

St. James Catholic Church established by French Capuchin priests in 1757 under the Bishop of Quebec. St.

James Parish was the site of the first Acadian settlement in Louisiana between 1756–1757. The Acadians followed along Hwy. 1 toward today's Thibodaux, west of Baton Rouge. The route was called the Acadian Trail.

St. James Landing
Mile 156.5, right bank descending ⚓

Vacherie
River mile 150

Two grand-nephews of Jean Baptiste Le Moyne de Bienville received a large land grant in this vicinity. Wealth in the new territory was often dependent upon which family you chanced to be born into. A *vacherie* is a dairy.

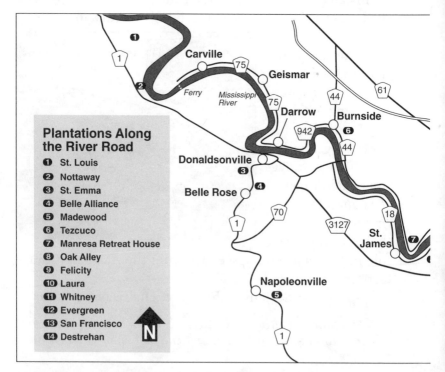

Plantations Along the River Road
❶ St. Louis
❷ Nottaway
❸ St. Emma
❹ Belle Alliance
❺ Madewood
❻ Tezcuco
❼ Manresa Retreat House
❽ Oak Alley
❾ Felicity
❿ Laura
⓫ Whitney
⓬ Evergreen
⓭ San Francisco
⓮ Destrehan

Oak Alley Plantation, Restaurant and B&B

3645 Hwy. 18, Vacherie, 800-442-5539, river mile 153.5.

This national historic landmark, built between 1837 and

1839, is famous for its alley of 28 live oak trees planted in perhaps 1770 by an early settler. Look for resurrection ferns growing on the branches

Oak Alley Plantation.

of the live oaks. Like Spanish moss, it is not parasitic.

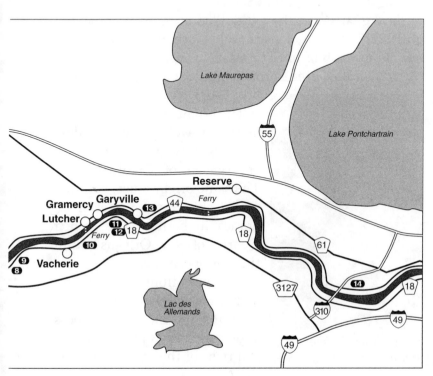

Laura: A Creole Plantation

2247 Hwy. 18, Vacherie, LA 70090, 225-265-7690 or 888-799-7690, www.lauraplantation.com. Admission $10. Guided tours daily 9:30 a.m. to 5 p.m.

Laura had 131,000 visitors last year, of which 34,000 were French-speaking. Plantation owner Norman Marmillion is a passionate guy with a background in film and puppetry. He has heavily researched his Creole gem, and he and his staff pride themselves on telling vivid stories of Laura and her family.

He says the main reason he saved the plantation was because the West African folktales of *Compain Lapin,* known in English as *Br'er Rabbit,* were recorded in the slave quarters at Laura and neighboring plantations. These centuries-old tales originated in Senegal in West Africa. Alcee Fortier first collected the stories in the 1870s. Alcee later became a dean at Tulane University and president of the American Folklore Society.

Slave quarters at the Laura Plantation were inhabited until 1977. In 2001, a visitor told Norman he had lived in one of those cabins until he was four years old. In the quarters, they called him Antoine. In New Orleans they called him Fats Domino.

Laura owner Norman Marmillion.

The bright colors of the Laura home, as well as the window shutters and expansive galleries, are typical of Creole homes. The same bright blues, yellows, pinks, and greens are seen on homes in both in the French Quarter of New Orleans and in the Caribbean today.

The main front door was seldom used by the French, who preferred the two small doors known as *brisees* just to the left and right of the main door. The

Laura Plantation.

raised open brick basement was typical of the Louisiana Creole style. Norman pointed out that the cypress logs for these homes were often pre-cut and numbered by skilled slave craftsmen. Rather like the Sears, Roebuck homes later ordered from catalogs!

Anglo-American plantations along the river (like Nottoway) have grand columns at the balcony entrance and were always painted white. It wasn't until the Creole French figured they were labeling themselves as second class to the wealthy Anglo-Americans that they started painting their colorful homes white and adding staircases and front doors to their homes to replace the *brisees*. Norman tells us that even though a large front door was added to the Laura home, it was kept locked until 1984!

Creole, he explained, is the non-Anglo (non-white Anglo-Saxon Protestant) culture that flourished before Louisiana became part of Anglo-America in 1803 with the Louisiana Purchase. For a Creole family, the plantation was not only "home" but also the business headquarters. Families had

to be active in the business to
live in the home.

Traditionally, the Creole plantation home (and the family
business) was passed on not to
the eldest child, but to the child
most likely to succeed in the
business. So in many cases, as
with the Laura Plantation, generations of owners were female.
Four generations of women ran
the Laura Plantation for 84 years
straight. A total of 82 children were born in the Laura Plantation home, and 52 of them married one another.

"Even today, I like to do business with a family I know,"
Norman admits. "Usually the first order of business is to
determine interrelationships of everyone's grandmother."

Forced heirship laws came into effect in 1824 as Ang-
los tried to find ways in which they could break up the
Creole family dynasties—the plantations that gave the Creole French an iron grasp on the best river soil. These laws
required that property be equally divided among all the
possible heirs.

According to Norm, a hundred years ago, 800 working
plantations were located between Natchez and New
Orleans. Of the many Creole plantations located along this
historic corridor, today only 8 remain.

Levee Road

As we continued down the Levee Road, we passed several deserted plantations where only a tangle of under-
brush marked the former location of grounds and gardens.
Notice that these are not wide properties. The "long lot"
platting seen in French settlements in Wisconsin, Illinois,
and Missouri was also practiced here. Long lots stretch-

ing out from the river assured each settler of access to the river and vital shipping.

We drove down the Levee Road early Christmas Eve to see bonfire foundations resembled log houses, triangles, circles, a star, and other shapes all along the levee. The bonfires are known to the Cajuns as *feux de joie,* and tradition suggests that they guide Santa to the homes along the river. In earlier days, the wood was gathered for weeks before the huge bonfires. Tall reeds known as *roseaux* created firecracker type explosions when added to the fire.

The levee in this vicinity is 30 or 40 feet high. Bedrock is buried beneath nearly one mile of silt. It is this deep layer of silt that makes bridge building much more difficult on the Lower river than it is on the Upper river.

In Vacherie (2155 Highway 18) we chanced upon one of our favorite Cajun fish shops, B & C Seafood Riverside Market and Deli—a real Cajun café where we had a meal of gumbo and enjoyed regional art on display. We spoke with fisherman and deli owner Tommy Breaux (see next page).

Feux de joie.

Tommy Breaux

Tommy is *Cajun* indeed and moved easily between speaking French and English. According to Tommy, authentic French-Canadian and Cajun languages are both archaic, carried to the new world in the middle 1600s from the county of Poitou in France.

The freezers at Tommy's market contained packages of fresh alligator, gar patties, turtle, crabmeat, oysters, catfish, and shrimp. There was even rabbit and raccoon meat selling for $15, $12, and $6 a package.

The ceilings are adorned with fish baskets, nets, fish traps, and other accouterments of the local culture. While the hoop nets are now illegal, Tommy said there was a time when he'd catch 2,500 to 3,000 pounds of fish with hoop nets in a day. A daily catch of 600 to 700 pounds is common among the fishermen that Tommy buys from today.

Most of the local crab and dressed fish are shipped to the East Coast. Tommy also harvests crawfish and eels, and his son specializes in crab. Eels are taken to market in Atlanta and shipped overseas by airplane—most likely to Holland or Sweden.

The salt-water intrusion has affected fishing during Tommy's lifetime. Lakes that used to yield freshwater catfish now yield red fish—a saltwater fish. Also, native freshwater fish are losing spawning grounds to salt water. Saltwater intrusion has been noticed as far inland as Lac des Allemandes.

Tommy also hunts alligators. Lease-holders are limited to harvesting a certain number of alligators—each over four feet long—per acre each year. For example, a 2,600-acre lease might allow for 40 alligators to be harvested. Tommy explained that an alligator hunt might reap 7 alligators in a day, and after a 10- to 14-day hunt he probably would have reached his yearly limit. He told us there's nothing quite like a load of alligators hissing and snapping in the back of a pickup truck!

ALLIGATOR DOS AND DON'TS

- It is illegal to feed or harass alligators or any other wildlife.
- Alligators are extremely agile both in and out of the water.
- Nesting females are the most aggressive.
- If you are threatened, make yourself as **tall** as possible, raising your hands above your head.

This alligator at Jean Lafitte Barataria Preserve is quite discernible in black and white but nearly invisible in living color.

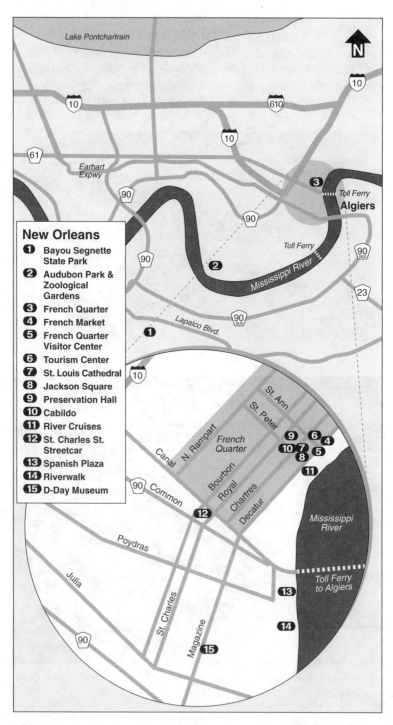

New Orleans

1. Bayou Segnette State Park
2. Audubon Park & Zoological Gardens
3. French Quarter
4. French Market
5. French Quarter Visitor Center
6. Tourism Center
7. St. Louis Cathedral
8. Jackson Square
9. Preservation Hall
10. Cabildo
11. River Cruises
12. St. Charles St. Streetcar
13. Spanish Plaza
14. Riverwalk
15. D-Day Museum

12

Greater City New Orleans

There is much to do in New Orleans. Eat well, play well! Enjoy jazz and blues around every corner. An extra evening in New Orleans allowed us to savor blues, jazz, exquisite oyster stew, Bananas Foster, and crayfish étoufféee, with our water's-edge hotel just a short drive from the French Quarter at Bayou Segnette State Park. Our visit lasted four days, and every day was full! The Audubon Aquarium, a dinner cruise on the Natchez paddlewheeler, long walks along the river, museums and historic sites. I strongly recommend a visit to **www.neworleansonline.com** for up-to-date options.

Parking near Harrah's Casino was $12 to $14 for the day. **Mulate's**, on Julia Street and Convention Center just outside the River Walk Shopping Complex, was recommended as a great Cajun Restaurant. We also ate in the French Quarter at the Café Masperos on 601 Rue Decatur Street. Its signature sandwich, the Muffaletta, is a local favorite for under $7, and the most expensive item on the menu is $9.50. A long line stretched along the walkway outside the entrance, but people were seated quickly.

VISITING NEW ORLEANS

While it is beyond the scope of this guidebook to list all the myriad attractions, restaurants, and cultural activities in the city of New Orleans, I can offer my personal top ten great things to do and see in New Orleans:

1. See it from the river!

The Steamboat Natchez. Toll free: (800) 233-2628, 2 Canal Street, Suite 2500. See the beauty and romance of New Orleans on a two-hour paddlewheel cruise starting at the heart of the French Quarter.

Riverboat John James Audubon. Toll free: (800) 233-2628, 2 Canal Street, Suite 2500. Four round-trip cruises daily between the Aquarium of the Americas and the Audubon Zoo.

Creole Queen and *Cajun Queen.* (504) 524-0814, 1 Canal Street. The 1,000-passenger paddlewheeler *Creole Queen* and the 600-passenger *Riverboat Cajun Queen* have docking facilities at Riverwalk and the Aquarium of the Americas.

2. Riverwalk and shops

Yep, right along the riverfront. Great spot to watch towering ocean freighters pass by. Hop on the ferry (free if you walk on) to Algiers—and easy access to several B&Bs that will cost you less than if you stay in the French Quarter.

3. Jackson Square and the Jackson Square Artist Community

Fronting the Mississippi in the heart of the French Quarter, the park is replete with hundreds of artists and musicians, shops, and such historic sites as the beautiful St. Louis Cathedral and the Cabildo (Louisiana State Museum site). Bounded by Chartres Street, St. Ann Street, and St. Peter Street.

4. Preservation Hall

726 St. Peter Street, (504) 522-284. New Orleans traditional jazz nightly.

5. Pat O'Brien's

718 St. Peter Street. One of the famous New Orleans piano bars.

Cabins at Bayou Segnette State Park.

6. Aquarium of the Americas and IMAX Theatre

Audubon Nature Institute, (504) 861-2537. Located on the Riverfront, at Canal Street and the edge of the French Quarter. At Aquarium of the Americas you'll see how the underwater world lives with lots of interesting exhibits.

7. Audubon Zoo

Audubon Nature Institute, (504) 861-2537, air@auduboninstitute.org. Approximately six miles south of the French Quarter, at 6500 Magazine Street. Take the St. Charles streetcar to the exit at Audubon Park and then the free shuttle to the zoo. One of the nation's finest zoos.

8. Confederate Museum

929 Camp Street, (504) 523-4522. For Civil War buffs this is a must-see.

9. Breakfast at Brennan's Restaurant

417 Royal Street. Classic fine dining in the French Quarter.

10. Bourbon Street and the French Quarter

Meander through through the old quarter with its bawdy bars, live music, and tasty foods.

National D-Day Museum

945 Magazine St. Entrance on Andrew Higgins Drive.

This museum was one of the final projects spearheaded by historian and author Stephen Ambrose. Plan two to four hours for your visit, as there are two 45-minute videos and much else to see. The 400 to 1,500 daily visitors see displays that include Home Front, Prelude to War, Planning for D-Day, and D-Day Beaches.

Higgins Industries in New Orleans built the landing craft used to transport troops, field artillery, and so on from the boats to the beaches during World War II. The designer, Andrew Jackson Higgins, had previously designed a similar boat, which could land against a shoreline without damaging its hull, for use in the swamps and marshes by oil companies, trappers, and fishermen.

Bayou Segnette State Park

7777 Westwego Blvd., Westwego, 504-736-7140, boat landing, RV parking, cabins on Bayou Segnette, just off Hwy. 90.

This well-maintained Louisiana State Park is remarkably close to the French Quarter in New Orleans. There is a very nice RV park with many large trees and pads at $12 a night for electric and water. The cabins here had screened porches and were built on stilts over the large waterway. It was an easy drive into the French Quarter and Canal Street from the park. Request directions and a free map at the ranger station.

Jean Lafitte National Historic Park and Preserve

7400 Hwy. 45 (Marrero, south of New Orleans). The Visitor Center is located at the Barataria Preserve.

A good map is available at the Visitor Center for the five smaller units of this park. There are over 20 miles of canoe trails in the preserve, and canoes can be rented from the nearby Bayou Barn. Winter, spring, and fall are the best seasons for exploring the bayous near the park—summers are hot, humid, and buggy.

INSIGHT

Salination (salt water incursion)

We had a fascinating conversation with the Interpretive Ranger at Jean Lafitte National Historic Park and Preserve about how Louisiana's fresh-water marshes and lakes are gradually becoming salinated now that flooding of the Mississippi is tightly controlled. Natural flooding of the Mississippi and the other rivers in Louisiana long served to deposit silt and fresh water over the land mass. Now that silt is no longer being deposited, the land is actually sinking.

A number of people told us that the double whammy of sinking and salination is the number one problem in Louisiana. As the ground water becomes more saline, fresh water grasses and vegetation die. Once standing water on private property reaches 18 inches deep year-round, the state reclaims that land. The sea is simply reclaiming southern Louisiana!

Besides causing salination, flood control also means that barrier islands are not being replenished with silt from the mainland. As they deteriorate, they no longer provide coastland with protection from hurricanes, so salt water encroaches farther inland and communities are more exposed to storms and storm surges.

A young alligator sunning itself on a log is well disguised.

There are several excellent walking trails in the 20,000-acre park. A boardwalk from the Visitor Center leads into a swamp of tupelo and baldcypress trees and then into a vast area of floating marsh. The marshes, mostly-composed of floating bogs of vegetation, are called *flotant (trembling ground)* in French.

Tupelos (a deciduous water-loving tree) are abundant along the trail beside Bayou Coquille *(shell)*. Notice the transition from tupelo swamps to the grassy marsh with sedges, rushes, and water plants that grow where trees cannot survive.

We heard a low rumbling at one point that could conceivably have been an alligator, though we could not find it. Later, we did see a fairly large gator sunning on a bank, but even the large ones are hard to see unless you know exactly where and what to look for. Amphibians, birds, and reptiles (including the venomous copperhead and water moccasin) can all be found along the trail, so bring your binoculars and camera—and use a stick, not your hand, if you need to clear away vegetation!

Bird sightings in the park the day we visited included great egret, belted kingfisher, pileated woodpecker, swamp sparrow, red-bellied woodpecker, snowy egret, glossy ibis, tufted titmouse, yellow-rumped warbler, ruby-crowned warbler, black-necked stilt, and turkey vulture, among many others.

Mosquitoes carrying the West Nile virus have been found in the New Orleans area. Wear long, loose, light-colored clothing with plenty of mosquito spray when outdoors. (Use a product with no more than 20 to 30 percent DEET.) The highest mosquito activity is at dawn and during early evening hours. There are over 60 species of mosquito in Louisiana.

Levees seen in this area are *hurricane* levees intended to protect residential areas from storm surges during hurricanes. Nearby Lake Cataouatche and Lake Salvador connect directly to the Gulf of Mexico.

INSIGHT

Jean Lafitte—A Robin Hood of the Bayous

Between 1812 and 1814, Lafitte was the leader of a gang of privateers and smugglers referred to as Baratarians. His men attacked Spanish ships (and others) in the Gulf of Mexico and the Caribbean for their cargo of slaves and luxury goods. The headquarters of the Baratarians was at Grand Terre on Barataria Bay in the Gulf of Mexico. Lafitte probably used Bayou des Familles and Bayou Coquille to transport plunder (normally slaves and goods) by pirogues from the Gulf to be sold cheaply to plantation owners. As smuggling was illegal, the goods and slaves were often auctioned, perhaps at high shell middons still seen in the park. Lafitte also provided supplies and men to General Andrew Jackson in the Battle of New Orleans against the British in 1815. This whole region became known as Lafitte country because of his activities here.

A peculiar feature of the natural distributaries or bayous is that they meander toward the sea on a *higher* elevation than their floodplains, constrained only by ridges or natural levees formed by the successive deposits of silt in repeated high-water periods. It is on these ridges that the earliest settlements developed. Without the continuous line of artificial levees along the Mississippi River, one third of Louisiana would flood annually during high water!

Native Indians in this area arrived about 2,000 years ago, attracted by the unusually large area of dry land and the diversity of animal and plant life within a relatively small area. Shell debris or "middons" left by Indian communities are common on this high land. Such middons, when placed on a natural levee, provided additional high, dry areas for natives to live on when the rivers flooded.

A Cajun Man's Swamp Cruise with Black Guidry

Give Black a call at 504-868-4625.

Our Louisiana explorations included a guided pontoon boat tour of the bayous just off the intercoastal waterway west of New Orleans with "Black" Guidry and his dog, Gator-bait. You'll see that our two tours of the Cajun backwaters were very different!

Dean Wilson (Wilderness Tours in the Atchafalaya Basin) and Black Guidry were both exceptionally knowledgeable about the river, and we enjoyed such wildlife as barred owls and horned owls, a white-faced ibis, little blue heron, and of course, alligators. For Cajun flavor though, you can't beat Guidry, who also played the accordion and guitar and sang "Ma Jolie Blonde" while Gator-bait howled an accompaniment.

**Follow Hwy. 23 south toward Venice and the end
of the Great River Road**

West Point à La Hache
Population 2,347

This site was named by the French—*Point of the Axe.* A map from 1765 labeled it "Hatchet Point." The main levee system on the east bank of the Mississippi River terminates at Pointe à La Hache, which is about 50 miles above the Head of Passes. In this vicinity, we found entire roadways paved with shells, and orange groves become quite common. A car ferry crosses the river between Point à La Hache and West Point à La Hache.

Woodland Plantation

21997 LA Hwy. 23 in West Pointe à La Hache on the Mississippi River, 800-231-1514.

Woodland Plantation (above) is depicted at right on the label of a bottle of Southern Comfort.

This is the home on the label of a bottle of Southern Comfort (see inset)! We found good birding along the levee behind the Woodland plantation home, and our memorable Christmas dinner at Woodland included seafood gumbo, stone crabs, shrimp, traditional turkey with oyster stuffing, and pecan pie with homemade ice cream.

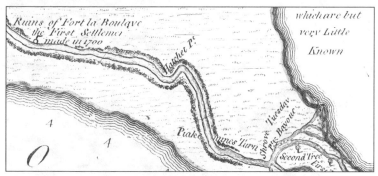

Lt. Ross map, 1775.

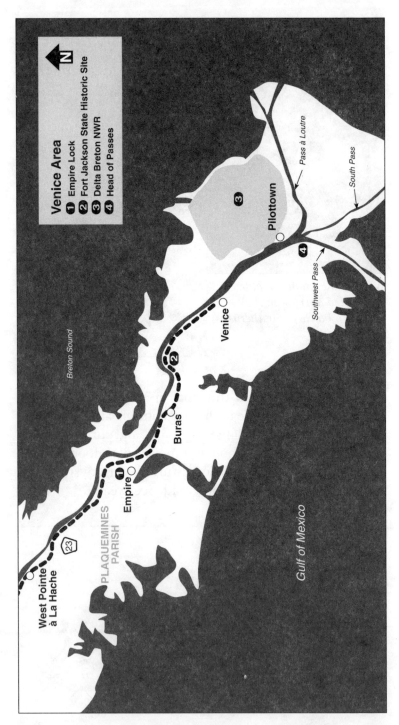

13

On to Venice!

Below Woodland Plantation, there is less and less habitable land along Highway 23, the route to Venice. The entire narrow peninsula was formed by silt deposits as the Mississippi pushed its delta into the sea. Lagoons along the road make it easy to observe waterfowl. Plantations front on the bayou, and cemeteries lie above ground.

Towns along the 67 miles between West Pointe à la Hache and Venice on Highway 23 are mostly nondescript settlements. Shrimp boats, ibis, and pelicans become abundant near Empire, and more oystering occurs here than farther south. There is an RV park near Buras.

Highway 23 was deserted when we traveled it in December, but the four lanes are necessary to provide a hurricane evacuation route for lower Louisiana. Levees here protect the area from hurricane storm surges—not high river stages.

This southern tip of Louisiana is endowed with petroleum, gas, sulphur deposits (produced at Port Sulphur), and rich resources of wildlife and fish.

Homeplace

Today this is just a small settlement, not much more developed than Captain Willard Glazier, who canoed the length of the Mississippi River in the 1880s, reported when he wrote of an overnight visit in "Home Place": *We had no choice but to occupy a sleeping-room with four other men and an equal number of dogs, the men being laborers in the orange groves. From this point, large quantities of oranges are shipped in sloops to New Orleans, which eventually find their way to the fruit stands and stores of Northern cities.*

Empire

Population 2,654.

Boats trolling for shrimp must move farther and farther out to sea—some as many as three miles out—as the closer shrimp beds are depleted. The boats you'll see with high rigging are the long-distance shrimping boats. Helicopters and crew boats cater to offshore oil rigs, moving men and supplies for repair and salvage work.

The **Empire Lock** at river mile 29.5 connects the Lower Mississippi with the Gulf of Mexico via Adams Bay. Vessels passing through the lock carry seafood, shells, and offshore oil drilling equipment and personnel.

Long-distance shrimp boats at Empire.

Buras
Population 6,383.

Orange groves are abundant here in the narrow strips of land between the road and the marshes abutting the sea. Locally grown satsuma, sweets and navel oranges, as well as ruby red grapefruit are offered for sale at roadside stands. Harvest was in full swing during our December visit. Waterfowl is abundant in the marshes beside the road.

Fort Jackson State Historic Site

River mile 18.6.

Named for Andrew Jackson, this almost-intact fort overlooks the Mississippi River at the mouth of Bayou Mardi Gras. Built between 1822 and 1832 to protect the Lower River, it withstood a 10-day siege by Admiral Farragut and his gunboats in 1862. The fort was manned until the 1920s.

A French fort was first erected here in the mid-1750s, and a Spanish fort was built in the same area in the 1790s. Bayou Mardi Gras was named in March 1699 by de

Fort Jackson

Oil rig diving bells.

Bienville and is the oldest named place of non-Indian origin in the whole Mississippi River Valley. The name disappeared from maps of the area until 1971, when it was restored.

Venice

River mile 10.8.
Population 2,220.

Suddenly we reached the southernmost town on the Great River Road that is accessible by automobile!

Most of Venice was destroyed by Hurricane Camille in 1969, when tidal surges and 200-mile-per-hour winds swept homes from Fort Jackson to Venice off their foundations.

The best birding is found offshore among various barrier islands, although we saw many waterbirds, including glossy ibis, stilts, herons, and egrets scattered in the lagoons along the roadway. Boats can be chartered for about $120 per person per day.

The levee still visible on the west bank of the river is the termination of what is likely the longest levee system in the world, extending north from Venice 650 miles to the Arkansas River.

When I arrived at Venice, my personal saga of travels along the Great River Road from the headwaters to the Gulf of Mexico—and sharing them with readers—reached its terminal point.

Delta/Breton National Wildlife Refuge

215 Offshore Shipyard Rd., Venice, at the lower tip of the Louisiana landmass. (Accessible by water only.)

Five thousand acres of barrier islands are included in the Breton National Wildlife Refuge, established in 1904. It was named a National Wilderness Area in 1975 to protect marshland and wilderness and to monitor oil and gas wells. Between the barrier islands of Louisiana's Gulf coast and

extending from 10 to 60 miles inland are 6.5 million acres of wetlands—40 percent of the nation's marsh ecosystem.

The area serves as a nesting colony for large colonies of terns, black skimmers, and gulls.

195

Head of Passes
River mile 0.0.

At this point, about 953.8 river miles below the confluence of the Ohio and Middle Mississippi Rivers, the Lower Mississippi comes to an end, branching into numerous small channels that lead into the Gulf of Mexico.

The passes through which the Mississippi River enters the Gulf of Mexico are not accessible by road, but it is possible for visitors to find a pilot who will run them out to Pilottown and the mouths of the Mississippi. We found that most pilots were asking about $120 per person. Keep in mind that birding and wildlife watching are the main rewards, as Pilottown has no visitor amenities.

The French began work on the shipping channels at the mouth of the Mississippi River as early as 1723, but for sailing ships, navigating the river to New Orleans remained a tortuous process that reportedly took nearly as long as the trip from Europe. Efforts to maintain a channel for ocean vessels continued through 1858, until James Buchanan Eads began his amazingly successful project—a series of jetties—in 1875. The jetty system he devised permanently deepened the channel to 30 feet (see sidebar on next page).

"At this point, about 953.8 river miles below the confluence of the Ohio and Middle Mississippi Rivers, the Lower Mississippi comes to an end, branching into numerous small channels that lead into the Gulf of Mexico."

INSIGHT

A Pilottown Ship Pilot's Job

At Fort Jackson, we spoke to Tania Booksh, whose husband is a ship's pilot who was stationed for two weeks at Pilottown. She and her children were meeting a boat that would take them out to Pilottown for the Christmas holiday.

Tania stressed that there are *no* visitor amenities in Pilottown. At one time the island had a school and some shops, but no longer. Today it strictly accommodates the ships' pilots stationed there, she explained. Then she reconsidered: "Well, on second thought, there *are* lots of alligators, owls, raccoons, turtles, and snakes in the marsh area."

As Tania explained it, the *ship's pilot* does not steer boats himself, but *directs* a foreign ship's pilot. River pilots may be certified for three parts of the River:
• from the mouth (Head of Passes) to Pilottown;
• from Pilottown to New Orleans;
• from New Orleans to Baton Rouge.

Pilot's Station *(now Pilottown)* and Mouths of the Mississippi, *painting by Henry Lewis.*

Captain James Buchanan Eads

It is not possible to finish this Mississippi River journey to the Gulf without a comment on James Buchanan Eads, for whom Port Eads at the very mouth of South Pass was named. The river buff is already familiar with Eads as the designer of the "impossible bridge" at St. Louis and the ironclad paddleboats used by the North in the Civil War.

It was this same Eads who developed and executed the concept of self-scouring jetties and other river works that allow ocean vessels adequate channel depth to approach New Orleans. He is considered to be among the top five engineers of all time, a group that includes Leonardo Da Vinci and Thomas Edison.

In 1829, when Eads was just nine years old, his parents moved from Indiana to Louisville, Kentucky. On board the steamboat, an engineer explained to him the principal parts of the ship's engine. At age thirteen, he and his family were marooned in St. Louis after a steamboat accident. He sold fruit on the street to help support his family until he began working with a business that allowed him access to an excellent library, where he studied books on mechanics, civil engineering, and physical science. By 1839 he was employed as a clerk on a steamboat. In 1842 he built a diving bell boat for salvage operations and worked the river from Galena to Balize, thus gaining a thorough understanding of the Mississippi riverbed.

In April 1861, three days after the Confederate attack on Fort Sumter, he was told to be ready on short notice to consult with the federal government about the Western rivers. Shortly afterward he submitted a plan to develop three ironclad boats to defend the waters out of Cairo, Illinois. In 1862, he was authorized to build six more ironclads, and he delivered them in 65 days.

From 1867 to 1874 Captain Eads constructed the steel-arch bridge at St. Louis, Missouri. The central arch of this bridge has a clear span of 520 feet and is considered to be the finest specimen of such a metal arch bridge in the world.

In his proposal of 1874 to deepen the Mississippi at the South Pass by means of jetties and other works, Eads was opposed by nearly the entire United States Corps of Engineers. When Congress approved allowing him to try his plan, the cost was to be $5.25 million, but payment would be granted in small increments as the channel actually deepened and widened itself—"No cure, no pay." The final million would be paid only after the river maintained a 30-foot depth throughout twenty years.

Eads was once more triumphant, and eventually received $8 million from the U.S. government. Work began in 1902 on similar structures for the Southwest Pass, and today ocean-going vessels bound for New Orleans or Baton Rouge use both passes. The U.S. Corps of Engineers maintains the channel, dredging when needed.

After this success, Eads was consulted about the bar at the mouth of St. John's River in Florida, the improvement of the Sacramento River, and improvement of the harbors of Toronto, Tampico, Galveston, and the estuary of the Mersey River in England.

Eads died in March of 1887 at the age of sixty-seven.

1859 Head of Passes map produced by the Mississippi River Commission*

Notice the Quarantine Station on the east bank of the Lower Mississippi and Pilot Station (now Pilottown) below. "Cubit's" house is approximately at Mile 0.0, and a hospital for lepers was located on Pass a Loutre. South Pass was the main navigation channel for ships bound for New Orleans out of the Gulf of Mexico.

* *Historic Names and Places, USACE*

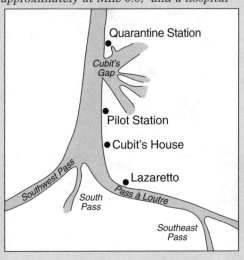

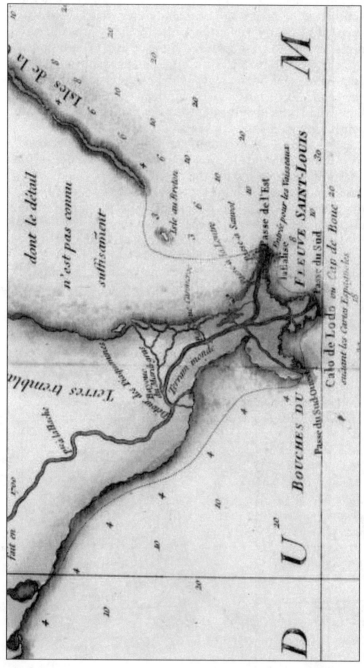

Jean-Baptiste Bourguignon d'Anville. "Carte de la Louisiane." 1732. The Tracy W. McGregor Library of American History.

Appendix

Tourism information below was accurate at the time of publication. Visit http://greatriver.com/lowertourism/ for updated web site and contact information.

ARKANSAS TOURISM CONTACTS
800-872-1259

Blytheville 870-762-2012
blygoscc@sbcglobal.net, www.blytheville.dina.org

Phillips County Chamber of Commerce (Helena Area) 870-338-8327
pcchamber@hnb.com, www.Phillips-County.com

Arkansas State Parks
888-AT-PARKS or www.arkansasstateparks.com

MISSISSIPPI TOURISM CONTACTS
800-927-6378

Mississippi DNR 601-961-5255

Tunica 601-363-2865

Clarksdale 800-626-3764

Greenville 800-467-3582

Vicksburg 800-221-3536

Port Gibson 601-437-4351

Natchez 800-647-6724

LOUISIANA TOURISM CONTACTS
800-695-1638

New Orleans Metropolitan Convention and Visitors Bureau
504-566-5005

St. Francisville Tourism Center
11757 Ferdinand St., St. Francisville, LA
Debra Credeur, 225-635-6769, cell 225-721-2354

New Roads Tourism Office
160 E. Main St., New Roads, LA
Tara Toney, 225-638-3998

Port Hudson State Historic Site
U.S. Hwy. 61, north of Baton Rouge
225-654-3775

Rural Life Museum
Essen Lane at Interstate 10, Baton Rouge, LA 70898
225-765-2437

River Road African American Museum
3138 Hwy. 44, Darrow, LA 70725
Kathe Hambrick, Curator, 225-562-7703

Plaquemines Parish Economic Development and Tourism Dept.
104 New Orleans Street, Belle Chase, LA
Pam Fields, Secretary, 504-394-0018

Visitor Center
1401 Carter St. (U.S. Hwy. 84), Vidalia, LA
318-336-7008

Baymont Inn—West Monroe (one of several motels in West Monroe)
503 Constitution Ave., West Monroe, LA 71292
318-387-2711

Birding in Louisiana

Turgeon Tours
Advertises "Dolphin and birding tours, down the bayou to the Gulf"
800-73-SWAMP, 504-689-2911

Lil' Cajun Swamp Tours
Cyrus Blanchard, 800-689-3213

Capt. Brent Guidry, Birding Tours
Cypress Cove, Venice, LA
504-912-1641

A Cajun Man's Swamp Cruise with Black Guidry
504-868-4625
Don't leave Louisiana without a swamp cruise. This Cajun man
plays accordion and guitar and has a singing dog named Gatorbait!
Good fun!

Last Wilderness Tours
Dean Wilson
www.lastwildernesstours.com
Call for appointment: 225-659-2499 or 225-692-4114

GUIDE TO RIVER MILES,
MEMPHIS TO HEAD OF PASSES

River miles for the Upper River are counted from Mile 0.0 at Cairo, Illinois, to Mile 839.0 at Lambert Landing in St. Paul, Minnesota. River miles for the Lower Mississippi are counted from 0.0 at Head of Passes (AHP), 90 miles below New Orleans to Mile 953.8 near Cairo, Illinois. By air, the distance from the mouth of the Ohio River to the Head of Passes is only 600 miles!

In the following River Mile notations, left and right designate the riverbank from the perspective of a boat *descending* the river. Official Army Corps of Engineers river charts are available, along with many other resources, at **greatriver.com**.

735.0 left	Memphis, Tennessee
687.6 left	Mhoon Landing, Mississippi
680.4 right	Whitehall Crevasse
672.3 right	St. Francis River
663.5 right	Helena, Arkansas
652.0 left	Friars Point, Mississippi
625.0	Sunflower Cutoff, vicinity of de Soto's discovery of the Mississippi River
599.0 right	White River mouth
585.0 left	Rosedale, Mississippi
584.0 right	Arkansas River mouth
565.0 right	Chicot Landing, Arkansas
560.5 left	Mound Landing, Mississippi. When the crevasse occurred here in 1927, Greenville was flooded and a 65-acre lake developed.
554.0 right	Arkansas City, Arkansas
537.2 left	Greenville, Mississippi
515.5 left	Lake Washington
496.5 left	Mayersville, Mississippi
487.3 right	Lake Providence, Louisiana
477.5	Fitler Bend
437.1 left	Vicksburg, Mississippi and Yazoo River
415.5 right	Davis Island, Mississippi
408.6 left	Big Black River
407.0 left	Grand Gulf, Misssissippi
396.2 right	St. Joseph, Louisiana
381.0 right	Waterproof, Louisiana. On the opposite bank is Ashland Landing, Mississippi, once the plantation of General Zachary Taylor who was elected President in 1849

363.8 left	Natchez, Mississippi and, at mile 363.3 right, Vidalia, Louisiana
326.0	Palmetto Bend
314.4	Old River Structures, Louisiana shore, help to control the flow of the Mississippi River into the Atchafalaya River basin
304.0 right	Old River Navigation Lock allows boats passage into the Red-Ouachita and Atchafalaya River systems.
302.8 left	Angola, Louisiana, State penal institution was established here in 1890.
265.5 left	St. Francisville, Louisiana. Pointe Coupée is located opposite.
256.0 left	Port Hudson, Louisiana
228.4 left	Baton Rouge and opposite, Port Allen Lock and Canal. Access to the Intracoastal Waterway.
208.6 right	Plaquemine, Louisiana
188.3 right	Claiborne Landing, Louisiana
185.1 left	Geismar, Louisiana
175.5 right	Bayou LaFourche and Donaldsonville, Louisiana. Opposite Darrow Louisiana.
156.5 right	St. James Landing, Louisiana
153.5 right	Oak Alley Plantation, Louisiana
150.0 right	Vacherie, Louisiana
146.4 left	Grammercy, Louisiana (home of Colonial Sugar Refinery)
120.0 left	Bonnet Carre Spillway is designed to protect New Orleans and its levees by diverting flood waters into Lake Pontchartrain.
95.0 left	New Orleans, Louisiana
47.0 right	Magnolia Plantation, Woodland is just above
45.0 left	Pointe à la Hache, Louisiana
29.5 right	Empire Lock
25.0 right	Buras, Louisiana
18.6 right	Fort Jackson, Louisiana (Historic Site)
10.8 right	Venice, Louisiana. Terminal point for the Great River Road. Opposite is "The Jump," the first channel or pass leading directly into the Gulf of Mexico.
3.0 left	Cubit's Gap, another permanent outlet of the Mississippi River.
0.0	*Head of Passes.* The Southwest Pass is most often used by oceangoing vessels that enter the Mississippi River from the Gulf.

THE CIVIL WAR IN THE SOUTH

Many issues divided North and South in the years leading up to the war between the states, often referred to in the south as the War of Northern Aggression. The issues included tariffs on imported goods, legalized slavery, and finally the conflict of Federal power vs. States' Rights.

While agriculture was the foundation of the American colony, there was a contrast in vision. The southern plantation economy was built on the backs of slaves. The North—which produced the plows that broke southern earth, the steamboats that carried their goods, and then purchased the cotton and other products produced on the plantations— thrived on entrepreneurship. The election of Abraham Lincoln, who believed that "a house divided against itself cannot stand," caused a crisis in the southern psyche that brought the differences between the two sections into sharp focus.[1]

Arkansas originally resisted the call to secede but joined the Confederacy following the attack on Fort Sumter. The battle of Pea Ridge, in March of 1862, was the first to be fought in northwest Arkansas.

The Vicksburg campaign branched into Arkansas twice during 1863, resulting in Confederate defeats at both Arkansas Post and Helena. There are excellent interpretive displays at both the Delta Cultural Center in Helena and the Arkansas Post National Memorial.

During the war, plantations were looted by Union soldiers. Confederate soldiers, too, needed supplies from the plantations. Those plantations that survived generally accommodated both Union and Confederate armies, often being used as hospitals or quarters for officers.

The war was devastating for most property owners in the South. In the Deep South in general, and while touring plantations in Natchez in particular, we learned of many a plantation owner who saw his fortunes melt away during and after the war.

Many plantation owners died shortly after the war, some quite possibly of broken hearts, leaving their wives without any income and huge properties and former slave populations to support. Notably, many of these women took on the added responsibilities quite stoically and competently after the deaths of their husbands. In some cases, several generations of former slaves continued to live on and "hold" property even after the white planters were forced to abandon the properties.

Mississippi and the Civil War

Some of the most bitterly contested battles in the war occurred in Mississippi. More than 772 military events took place there. The 47-day siege of Vicksburg, during which citizens dug into the bluffs to escape the terrifying bombardment, was one of the longest in history. Jefferson Davis, a planter and resident of Warren County (near Greenville), was elected president of the Confederate States of America. The *Cairo*, one of the North's "ironclad" boats, has been raised from the Yazoo River and is (intermittently) on display in Vicksburg.

Once one of the wealthiest states, Mississippi was laid waste and has remained one of the nation's poorest states ever since. Must-see battlefields include the monuments of the Vicksburg National Military Park. Near Port Gibson, don't miss Grand Gulf Military Park, and the ruins of Windsor—the largest antebellum mansion built in Mississippi.[2]

Louisiana and the Civil War

The **Port Hudson State Commemorative Area Civil War Battlefield** is on Highway 61, five miles south of St. Francisville. The battlements are still visible. There is an excellent interpretive center with a computer that will spit out the name and status of Civil War soldiers for any given surname.

The Battle of Port Hudson was one of the first in which freed slaves serving as soldiers engaged in combat on the side of the Union. During the Civil War, more than 24,000 blacks from Louisiana joined the Union army—the largest black contingent from any state. A total of 300,000 blacks served in the U.S. army and navy during the Civil War, sixteen of whom were awarded the Medal of Honor. Port Hudson surrendered on July 9, 1863, five days after the fall of Vicksburg. It was the last link between the two sides of the Southern Confederacy. The Confederacy could not stand divided.

Civil War displays in New Orleans include the **Cabildo,** part of the **Louisiana State Museum,** the **United States Customs House, Butler's first headquarters,** and the **Old U.S. Mint. Confederate Memorial Hall** (noted on New Orleans city maps) contains one of the largest collections of Confederate artifacts. The **Metairie Cemetery** is the final resting place of three Confederate generals: P.G.T. Beauregard, Richard Taylor, and John Bell Hood. General Leonidas Polk is buried at **Christ Church Cathedral** on St. Charles Avenue.[3]

For information on the **Civil War Discovery Trail,** call 800-298-7878.

A BRIEF HISTORY OF THE ACADIANS
IN LOUISIANA: THE GRAND DERANGEMENT[4]

- In the 1750s, Jesuits began growing sugar cane near New Orleans. In 1795 a planter named De Bore succeeded in crystallizing cane juice. By the time of the Civil War, Louisiana supported over 1,500 sugar mills. From 1910 to 1920, sugar cane diseases, anthrax, and falling prices collapsed the sugar industry and the great plantations. The Great Depression followed shortly after.

- In 1755, the Acadians were expelled from Nova Scotia during the war between France and England. Their farms were seized, and families, many separated in the confusion, were sent to the thirteen American colonies, often as indentured "slaves" to businessmen who financed their passage on ships. Gradually, over a period of 10 years, families migrated to the wetlands of French Louisiana in a movement now called the *Grand Derangement*.

- In 1765, the first Acadians arrived in La Louisianne.

- Cajun culture is established: By the mid-1800s, many Acadians had joined fishermen and smugglers living on barrier islands and estuaries or marshlands. Skills learned on seaside dikes in Canada's Acadia translated well to the seashores of Louisiana.

- In 1791, Black slaves revolted in Saint-Dominique (today's Haiti). Ten thousand Creoles immigrated to Louisiana between 1791 and 1803.

- In 1803, slavery revolts and European wars finally prompted Napoleon Bonaparte to abandon French Louisiana to America.

- In 1815 the Battle of New Orleans took place. Andrew Jackson led many Acadians and Creole French to victory over the British. The legendary privateer Jean Lafitte contributed to the American effort by providing Jackson with men and supplies.

- Between1820 and1860, "cotton was king, but sugar ruled." Steamboats and railroads triggered a boom in production on plantations.

- From 1861 to 1865 the Civil War raged across the South.

- In 1901, oil was discovered in Louisiana.

- In 1916, the Louisiana state board of education forbade the speaking of French in public schools.

- In 1965, teachers from France, Canada, and Belgium were brought into Louisiana classrooms to reinstate the teaching of French. French-speaking culture was revitalized. By the late 1980s, "Cajun is Chic!"

KEY PLAYERS IN THE EXPLORATION OF NEW FRANCE

Rene-Robert Cavelier de La Salle was born in France in 1643. During the spring of 1681 La Salle, his Lieutenant Henri de Tonti, 23 Frenchmen, 18 Indian men, 10 women and 3 children set out from the mouth of the Ohio for the Gulf. They reached the Gulf one year later and La Salle claimed the entire region drained by the Mississippi for the country of France.

With this proclamation, France acquired all the land bordered by the plains of Texas, the Rocky Mountains, the Allegheny Mountains, and the vast basin of the Mississippi River from north to south.

La Salle then immediately returned to France, where Louis XIV commissioned him to return in 1684 to establish a colony at the mouth of the Mississippi. La Salle, however, was unable to find it again. He landed his ship along the Texas coast and proceeded to march east.

Before reaching the Mississippi, his men mutinied and killed him. La Salle had left his partner, Henri de Tonti, at the mouth of the Arkansas River to hold the French claim to the Mississippi River. Tonti waited four years before leaving six men to hold the fort on the Arkansas Post while he searched for La Salle.

Pierre Le Moyne, Sieur d'Iberville, continued the search for the mouth of the Mississippi River under the command of Comte Pontchartrain. In January 1699, d'Iberville first saw Spanish galleons near today's Pensacola. He gradually moved westward along the coast until March 2, when, accompanied by his brother and a priest, he discovered a river "all muddy and white," which he believed to be the Mississippi River.

To prove that he had indeed found the Mississippi, d'Iberville continued up river with his longboats in an effort to find an eastern fork in the river and an Indian village specifically mentioned by La Salle in his journals. In his journal is a reference to a red stick *(baton rouge)* which marked the boundary between the hunting grounds of the Ouma and Bayogoula Indians. It was probably a high tree, stripped of limbs, painted red, and hung with fish heads and bear bones as a sacrifice.

Just south of today's Pointe Coupée and a large Ouma village, d'Iberville discovered a river flowing directly east. The party split, with d'Iberville and four Canadians following the Fork (named River Iberville) while his brother and the forty-four men returned south on the Mississippi to the Gulf. The Iberville River led to Lakes Maurepas and Pontchartrain, then to the Gulf.

The two groups reunited on March 31, 1699. On his return, d'Iberville displayed a letter from Henri de Tonti to La Salle that he had secured from an Indian chief. This letter proved conclusively that the great river was indeed La Salle's Mississippi. Iberville established a fort at Biloxi Bay and sailed out in the Gulf for France.[5]

In 1760, after French settlers attempted an uneasy settlement among the Natchez Indians, **Antoine Cadillac[6] de La Mothe,** then the royal governor of Louisiana, offered d'Iberville his daughter's hand in marriage. It was not a happy offer from Cadillac, who scorned d'Iberville as a mere adventurer and Canadian.

D'Iberville respectfully declined the offer. In retaliation, Cadillac equipped him with 34 men and ordered him to the Natchez settlement to build a fort and punish the Indian "murderers."

Although dismayed to be ordered to conquer a tribe of 800 warriors with only 34 men, d'Iberville managed to strike a treaty, beheaded two Indians known to have killed Canadians, and then enlist the natives to help him build Ft. Rosalie. He returned in triumph to continue governing New Orleans.

A few short years later, Cadillac stopped in at Natchez on a hunt for silver and gold only to reignite old hostilities. In 1729, the Natchez Indians massacred most French settlers in the Natchez country. The continuing war with French soldiers practically annihilated the Natchez as a nation.[7]

Jean Baptiste Le Moyne, Sieur de Bienville[8] was nineteen when he began the journey from the Gulf of Mexico to Pointe Coupée in 1699 with his brother d'Iberville. Much of his life was spent as governor of the territory. In September 1718, he reported that he was at work on the new city of New Orleans, as directed by "The Company of the West." In 1721 the Vieux Carre (Old Quarter) was laid out, and later that year, a census showed 470 people lived in the area, of whom 194 were slaves.

Comte Pontchartrain, Minister of the French Navy, ordered d'Iberville to rediscover the mouth of the Mississippi River and select a site, easily defended, from which entry to the river by other nations could be blocked.

John Law was a Scottish financier and adventurer, a contemporary of d'Iberville and Bienville at the dawn of the eighteenth century. In 1717, Law's Company of the West was appointed to manage the royal colony of Louisiana by French king Louis XIV. Law was a flagrant promoter and drew some 7,000 European settlers, including convicts and indentured servants, to the Mississippi River Delta. Because Law's company purchased the Company of Senegal, which held a French monopoly on the slave trade, Law also brought nearly 3,000 black slaves from Africa between 1720 and 1731.

When Law's scheme, referred to as the *Mississippi Bubble,* burst some years later, it was de Bienville who convinced the Germans who had hoped to settle on Law's property to resettle north of his new village of New Orleans. Some 150 Germans settled in what is today referred to as the "German Coast" in the vicinity of Geismar, mile 185.1 along the left bank.

The goal of **Louis XIV** was to control the river valley fur trade and provide a base of defense against Spanish and English encroachment into the Mississippi River Delta. John Law had great influence in the court of Louis XIV, having established the new national bank in France. Law's failed Company of the West was the major asset of the infant French National Bank.

Jesuit priests belonging to the Society of Jesus were active in the early settlement of the entire Mississippi River valley, from Canada to the Gulf. Père Marquette (shown) was himself a Jesuit priest. De Bienville and d'Iberville included a Jesuit in their initial foray up the Mississippi in 1699. The Jesuits often traveled alone among the Indian villages in the great expanse of wilderness and endured incredible hardships. In addition to establishing missions and educational institutions, the Jesuits helped to introduce indigo, oranges, figs, and sugar cane to the settlements along the Louisiana delta.

The order was expelled from the New World in 1763 because of European opposition to it. They were not allowed to return until 1837.

SUMMARY OF MISSISSIPPI RIVER BRIDGES[9]

More than two hundred bridges cross the Mississippi River, and only seventeen of them (including both railroad and highway bridges) cross the Lower river. It was not until 1898 that adequate technology allowed for building supports into the mile-plus-deep silt of the Lower Mississippi.

Crescent City Connection Bridges, U.S.-90 Alternate
The Greater New Orleans Bridge is 95 miles from the Mississippi river's mouth and has the longest spans and the highest vertical clearance of any bridge on the Mississippi River. It ranks second in the United States, fifth in the world!

Huey P. Long Railway/Highway Bridge, New Orleans, I-90
Built in 1935, its combined 4.5-mile approaches make this the longest continuous structure of any kind in the world.

Hale Boggs Bridge, Luling, LA I-310
A cable-stayed design with two A-shaped towers. Finished in 1983 and constructed to withstand hurricane forces from the Gulf of Mexico—a first for this kind of span. Look for the three-spiral ramp to the ground. Highly unusual!

Gramercy/Wallace Highway Bridge, LA
The steel for this bridge was shipped in from Japan and Korea.

The "Sunshine Bridge," Donaldsonville, LA SR 70
This bridge (at right) was named for the song "You are My Sunshine," co-written by Governor James H. Davis in the 1940s. Set 167.5 miles above the mouth, the bridge was maligned as the "bridge that went nowhere." It started on the west bank and ended in sugar cane fields on the east. Today, the towns of Donaldsonville and Union are at either end of the bridge and the bridge is credited with significantly increasing development on the eastern shore.

Borace Wilkinson Bridge, Baton Rouge, LA I-10

This double kingposted truss bridge is six lanes wide and was completed 1967. It is the last bridge under which ships can travel. Like previous bridges, its main span is over the deepest part of the river. It is symmetrical, but is askew of the river.

Huey P. Long Highway/RR Bridge, Baton Rouge, U.S. I-90

South of this bridge, the river is 40 feet deep or more, but just north of it, the depth is only 12 feet at most. As many as one thousand men worked to build this bridge.

Natchez, Mississippi, Highway Bridges U.S. 65

The piers are a total of 375 feet high from the bottom of the pier to the top of the superstructure. One hundred feet are in water an another 70 in river silt. The Mississippi side has a high bluff, but on the Louisiana side, note the long approach required. Ferries carried travelers across the river for 150 years before the first bridge was built here in 1940.

Helena, Arkansas, Highway Bridge U.S. 49

The superstructure of the Helena Bridge is long—3,108 feet long! There are five spans of multiple cantilevered trusses, most of which are visible only from a towboat.

Greenville, Mississippi, bridge, U.S. 82

Located 7 miles from Greenville, the Mississippi side has a 1-mile approach. Piers are sunk 180 feet below the water's surface—100 feet in water, the rest in silt. When a tow full of lead sank there in 1963, it was immediately completely buried in the silt.

Vicksburg Highway/Railway Bridge, U.S. 80

Completed in 1930 and supplanting a ferry service, this is another truss bridge with two anchor spans. It is unique in that the railroad tracks run right next to the highway rather than on a separate level. A strong cross-current at this point makes it one of the most dangerous bridges on the river for towboat captains.

Vicksburg I-20 Bridge

Completed in 1973. While this looks like an older truss bridge, it is in fact wider, stronger, and of a more simple design. I-beams are used throughout, rather than holed or trussed beams.

BOOK LIST

Along the River Road
Mary Ann Sternberg, © 1996 by Louisiana State University Press.

Mississippi River Panorama
William J. Petersen. Paintings by Henry Lewis, 1845–1849.

Down the Great River
© 1887 by Willard Glazier, Hubbard Bro. Publishers.

Reelfoot and the New Madrid Quake
Juanita Clifton as told to Lou Harshaw, © 1980 Victor Publishing Co.

The Great River Caper
Ed Wright, ©1995.

The Mighty Mississippi
Lori Erickson, © 1995, Globe Pequot Press.

River World
Virginia S. Eifert, © 1959, Dodd, Mead & Co.

Historic Names and Places on the Lower Mississippi River
U.S. Army Corps of Engineers, © 1977.

Climbing the Mississippi River Bridge by Bridge
Mary Charlotte Aubry Costello, © 1995.

Rising Tide: The Great Mississippi Flood of 1927 and How It Changed America
John M. Barry, © 1997.

Off the Beaten Path: Mississippi
Marlo Carter Kirkpatrick.

NOTES

1 Brochure, *Thousand Mile Front*, Civil War in the Lower Mississippi Valley.

2 Ibid.

3 Ibid.

4 Acadian Culture Center in Thibodaux.

5 Glen Morgan, Pointe Coupée Historical Museum exhibit.

6 For more on Cadillac's exploits on the Mississippi River, see Vol. 3, *Discover! America's Great River Road.*

7 *Down the Great River,* Willard Glazier, 1887.

8 Painting by Rudolph Bohunek (c. 1875–); 1910 oil on canvas, Louisiana State Museum.

9 Bridge notes are taken from *Climbing the Mississippi River Bridge by Bridge* by Mary Charlotte Aubry Costello in two voumes. Volume 1 includes detailed sketches and notes on all the bridges on the Lower River. Available for sale at **www.greatriver.com.**

Index

About the Author

Pat Middleton is a writer, publisher, and lecturer living along the Mississippi River near La Crosse, Wisconsin. Pat is a frequent guest lecturer aboard the great steamboats cruising the Mississippi River and contributes regularly to many midwestern and national magazines. Her Mississippi River Home page at **greatriver.com** is ranked as the most-visited Mississippi River travel, birding, and educational resource on the Web.

Recent river trips on the Yangtze River, the Amazon, the St. Lawrence Seaway, the Columbia River, and the Canal du Midi are detailed at **greatriver.com/waterwaycruises.**

Pat speaks throughout the Midwest to educators, writers, schoolchildren, historians, travel groups, and radio and television audiences, sharing her enthusiasm about her craft and the great Mississippi River, its heritage and natural history.

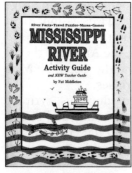

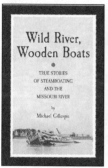
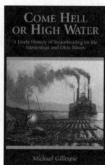
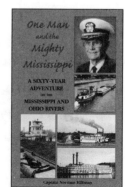

Also from Great River Publishing:

Poster-sized Map of the entire Great River Road
with notes on towns along the river $7.95

The River Companion by Karen "Toots" Maloy.
An excellent primer for first-time boaters on the great river .
$7.95

Official navigation charts for the entire Illinois,
Upper and Lower Mississippi Rivers . . . . Call for pricing

Marina/Amenities listings
for the entire Mississippi River $15.00

River Excursion Notecards
Exubernt original artwork; 7-pack of variety notecards
and envelopes. See at **www.greatriver.com** $12.95

**Hand-painted and Antiqued Mississippi
and Missouri River Maps**
Signed and numberd by artist. We have seven
varieties in all sizes, in the original French,
English, and Spanish. Also one ribbon map
of the entire river dated 1887. Maps can be seen
at . . . . **www.greatriver.com/oldmaps**

To order any of our products,
call Heritage Press toll-free at

888-255-7726

or order securely online at

www.greatriver.com/order.htm

You may also order any of our books
by mailing your personal check or money order to

Heritage Press
W987 Cedar Valley Road
Stoddard, WI 54658

Please include $3.95 shipping with your order.